The Love of Gardening

The Love of Gardening

EDITED BY KENNETH A. BECKETT

with contributions from

**Gillian Beckett · Kenneth A. Beckett · Ann Bonar
Julia Clements · H.J. Dodson · J.R.B. Evison · S. Miller Gault
Richard Gorer · J.R. Hare · Jack Harkness · Roy Hay
Arthur Hellyer · Anthony Huxley · Frank Knight
John G. Scott Marshall · Horace Parsons · Noel J. Procter
P.S. Stagg · Philip Swindells · R.E. Thoday
Percy Thrower · Peter Wood**

Line drawings by Rosemary Wise

With a Foreword by **HRH Princess Alice, Duchess of Gloucester**

CASSELL
LONDON

CASSELL LTD.
35 Red Lion Square, London WC1R 4SG
and at Sydney, Auckland, Toronto, Johannesburg,
an affiliate of
Macmillan Publishing Co., Inc.,
New York.

First published 1980

ISBN 0 304 30769 6

Photoset by Inforum Ltd, Portsmouth, England

Printed and bound in Great Britain by
Fakenham Press Ltd,
Fakenham, Norfolk

CONTENTS

FOREWORD

KENSINGTON PALACE

England has long held a high reputation among the world's great gardening nations. This has been sustained over the centuries by such names as 'Capability' Brown, William Robinson and Gertrude Jekyll. They were the prime preservers – and the cultivators too – of a precious heritage which has been tended down the years by those many gardeners who, in private estates and public parks, have dedicated themselves to this demanding profession. Often ill-rewarded financially, their satisfaction has been the sustaining of a living tradition.

The Gardeners' Royal Benevolent Society takes tremendous care and interest in the welfare of the gardeners themselves and their wives and widows; sparing them as far as possible the financial anxieties of old age. As their President I have been privileged to see how well they succeed. It is therefore a particular pleasure for me to introduce a book which combines one of my closest interests and this most deserving of organizations. The garden at Barnwell Manor has been for many years a source of great pleasure to me and likewise gardens overseas in Australia, Kenya and other places.

The Love of Gardening brings together some of the finest gardeners working and writing in this country today, whose charming yet eminently helpful essays should delight enthusiasts of all ages. This book will, I know, give pleasure to many and, fittingly, its success will benefit those who have done so much to maintain the English garden at its best.

President
The Gardeners' Royal Benevolent Society

ABOUT THE CONTRIBUTORS

Gillian Beckett, a geographer and teacher with a keen interest in horticulture and botany, was formerly a council member of the Botanical Society of the British Isles. She is the co-author of books on planting native trees and shrubs and indoor plants.

Kenneth Beckett spent 25 years as a practical gardener before taking up the pen to earn a living. A former assistant curator of the Botanic Gardens in Glasgow and technical editor of *Gardeners' Chronicle*, he is now a freelance editor and technical consultant on horticultural and botanical matters. Over the years he has written hundreds of articles on plants, an encyclopaedia of gardening, the *Illustrated Dictionary of Botany*, as well as books on trees, shrubs and greenhouse plants.

Ann Bonar is a freelance writer, journalist and editor. Her wide experience in the field of horticulture includes a period as a market gardener, as garden advisor at Fison's garden centre, as a lecturer, and 11 years answering readers' letters for *Amateur Gardening*. She has recently published the *St. Michael Guide to Houseplants* and a three-volume *Seasonal Guide to Gardening*, and is currently working on several books on horticultural subjects.

Julia Clements (Lady Seton in private life) is one of the foremost British flower arrangers. She is founder of the Modern School of Floral Art and has written 18 best-selling books on the subject. She has judged and demonstrated flower arranging all over the world and appears on television and radio. Three roses have been named in her honour.

Harry Dodson holds the position of head gardener at the Chiltern Gardens in Hungerford. Brought up on the Blackmoor Estate of the Earl and Countess of Selborne, where his uncle was head gardener, his interest in gardening dates from an early age. He trained further at Stansted Park Gardens and Ashburnham Place, and was for a time general foreman at Keigh Park Gardens, and at Mareham Park, before taking up his present post in 1947.

Raymond Evison, formerly Director of Parks, Brighton, has long been one of the ablest exponents of public parks policy. He is a past President of the Institute of Parks and Recreation Administration, and a Vice-President of the Royal Horticultural Society. He has written several books, including *Gardening by the Sea* and *Saturday in My Garden*.

Simpson Miller Gault trained in some of the finest private gardens, including Cliveden, and spent the last 40 years of his career as Superintendent of Regional Parks. A fine all-rounder, he is equally at home in the vegetable garden or among his favourite roses. He is author or co-author of several books, including one on trees and shrubs.

Richard Gorer started writing in 1959 when he was asked by Thomas Rochford to collaborate in *The Rochford Book of House Plants*. Since then he has written numerous articles on various aspects of gardening. Of recent years he has tended to concentrate on the historical aspects of gardening and on the activities of the various plant collectors.

John Hare was formerly Bailiff of the Royal Parks, a post which gave him overall jurisdiction over all the royal parks of London. He retired in 1979 and now acts as part-time horticultural consultant. He was trained in private gardens, including Kirklington Hall, Melmerby Hall and Newby Hall in Yorkshire, as well as at the Royal Botanic Gardens, Edinburgh. In 1962 he took up the position of Senior Superintendent of the Central Parks of London, and was appointed Bailiff in 1972.

Jack Harkness, rose grower and author extraordinaire, has spent his life rose-growing and breeding and has done much to further the popularity of the rose. He also writes with enthusiasm about his favourite subject and has written many articles and a book on the rose.

Roy Hay, a former editor of *Gardening Chronicle*, is also the author of several books and many articles and is gardening correspondent for *The Times*. He also acts as a consultant for many publishers, and was the consulting editor for the best-selling *Readers' Digest Encyclopaedia of Garden Plants and Ferns*.

Arthur Hellyer, former editor of *Amateur Gardener*, is the co-author of many books on gardening, covering all aspects of the subject. He is also a keen plantsman, with gardens in Sussex and the Channel Islands. For many years he has been gardening correspondent for the *Financial Times*.

Anthony Huxley, former editor of *Amateur Gardening*, is best-known as the author of almost 20 books on varying aspects of gardening and botany, including the popular *Mountain Flowers* and *Plant and Planet*. He has travelled extensively and was one of the first botanist/gardeners to visit China when the bamboo curtain was lifted recently.

Frank Knight was formerly Director of the Royal Horticultural Society's garden at Wisley and several other noteworthy horticultural establishments, as described in his autobiographical essay.

John Scott Marshall, formerly editor of *Gardening Chronicle* and the Ministry of Agriculture, Fisheries and Food publications on horticulture, has a keen interest in garden history and much enjoys visiting gardens. He has a noteworthy garden of his own – Hill Pasture in Essex – that is on occasion open to the public.

Horace Parsons trained in private gardens and nurseries, including Wakehurst Place, Tilgate Garden and Orwoods. Although a fine all-round gardener, he is perhaps best known for his expertise in fruit and vegetable growing. In 1952 he was appointed head gardener of the Royal Estate, Sandringham. He is also the author of *Grapes Under Glass*, and has written many articles on other gardening topics.

Noël Prockter, formerly editor of *Amateur Gardening*, trained at Lingfield, Cheal's of Crawley, and as a student gardener at the Royal Botanical Gardens, Kew. HIs literary output includes three books on horticulture, *Simple Propagation*, *Garden Hedges* and *Climbing and Screening Plants*. Now retired, he still works as a freelance writer.

Peter Stagg, having trained at the royal parks and the Royal Horticultural Gardens, Wisley, became head gardener at Bexley in 1956. In 1958 he took up the position of Deputy Superintendent of Parks, Cemeteries and Allotments for the Borough of Bexley. He is at present Superintendent of Parks and Gardens for the City of London Corporation, a post he has held since 1965.

Philip Swindells studied horticulture at Cambridge University Botanic Gardens. His commercial experience includes a spell spent working at the famous old nursery of Perry's at Enfield. He then moved to Scotland, to Castle Kennedy Gardens, and is currently superintendent of the Northern Horticultural Society's garden at Harlow Car, Harrogate. He has written several books on gardening, is a regular contributor to the horticultural press and has appeared on radio and television.

Ralph Thoday was, until his retirement, head gardener of the grounds of King's College, Cambridge. A fine all-round gardener/plantsman, during his career he was much in demand as judge and lecturer. The Royal Horticultural Society recognized his talents by awarding him the Victoria Medal of Horticulture in 1973.

Percy Thrower, the first radio and television gardening 'impresario', is possibly still the most familiar gardening expert to millions of enthusiasts all over the British Isles. He is much less well known for his other role as Superintendent of Shrewsbury Parks, a post from which he recently retired. He is now part-owner of Murrell's rose nursery near Shrewsbury.

Peter Wood trained at the Royal Horticultural Garden, Wisley. His prime ambition was to become editor of *Amateur Gardener*, a position he now ably holds. Not merely a journalist, he is also a keen craftsman with a special interest in growing the less hardy plants outside.

The
Pulse of Life

Anthony Huxley, V.M.M.

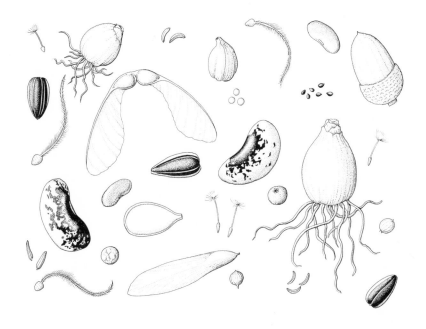

C ONSIDER a pinch of seed . . . It is usually impossible to tell them apart, especially the really tiny ones like begonia, gloxinia or calceolaria; the same is true of many bigger seeds, say those of cabbages, cauliflowers or kohl rabi, or those of the multitudes of annuals. No doubt some experts can recognize some of these, but it would be a brave expert who would attempt to sort out a mixture.

Yet each of these seeds will produce a different adult plant. In the hand one can hold a blaze of summer colour, a dish of salad, succulent tomatoes, a future forest – or of course also a mass of weeds. This is one of those miracles of nature which the gardener, with the plant name on the packet, takes for granted.

Of course we all know about evolution and genes nowadays, and how the seeds can hold that genetic code which allows one dust-like speck to grow into *Petunia* 'Giant All-Double', and another into *Begonia* 'Thousand Wonders Red'. It is salutary to remember that little more than a century ago botanists as eminent as Hooker and Arnott could preface a *Flora* with the words 'Many species . . . were simultaneously called into existence on the third day of creation, each distinct from the other and destined to remain so'. I suppose breeding as complex as that behind some of our garden plants today would have been impossible even to speculate on in that climate of belief.

It is almost as amazing that these tiny seeds can grow into quite large plants, even though almost all seeds (orchids are the notable exceptions) contain, besides the embryo plant and its gene-holding nucleus, some reserve of food for the minuscule organism which, on germination, makes what must often be an amazing struggle to establish itself. No plant in nature can choose where it will grow, and some gardeners are not as thoughtful as they might be when they sow. Think of the seed's microscopic roothairs trying to force themselves into or between great hard lumps of soil for toe-hold and life-giving moisture – and perhaps take more care the next time you draw out a seed-drill!

There is something irresistible to me about strange seeds and I tend to collect them both when garden-visiting and on travels abroad – even if I know they are unlikely to prove very satisfactory to me in the long run. What really is the point of my trying to germinate seeds of *Magnolia campbellii* or *Davidia* when I have a relatively small garden? Well, I could always give the seedlings away, and my choice is not always stupid – for example, *Magnolia wilsonii*, now 2 ft high from seed, should make quite a nice plant in a few years.

There is no doubt that trees grown from seed are specially prized by the gardener who has done so. The potential of a tree seed is the most remarkable of all. For example, a seed of giant redwood weighing less than 1/500 of a gramme can develop into a tree with a volume of 1,500 cubic metres and a weight of over a thousand tonnes – an increase of around 250,000 million!

Certainly exotic seeds are always tempting, especially if they are of plants not likely to be available at nurseries. Leaving aside odds and ends from tropical rain-forests which languish in a propagator, a few of my exotics have been quite rewarding. Twice, for instance, I had seen in central Turkey the splendid vivid yellow-flowered *Rosa raphinii* (the single origin, it is believed, of *R. hemisphaerica*). Years later I was there in autumn, and recalled a fine bush I had photographed on a certain corner of a certain road. Yes, there it was, covered with blackish heps; a handful of these was collected, brought home, sown, and after four years I have some sizeable bushes whose flowering I await impatiently.

I may be the only person in Britain with *Rosa raphinii* in my garden, and I am fairly certain I am alone in having plants of the almost protea-like, orange-flowered shrubby *Chuquiraga jussieui* from the higher slopes of Cotopaxi in the Ecuadorian Andes – in this case raised from seeds which fell out of the pressed specimen I brought home for identification.

There is the same can't-resist magic in the bulbs and other underground storage organs which seem to have become the main target of plant collectors of late, being relatively easy to bring home. No supermarket prepack is as well devised as a crocus corm, say, in its husky coat, a blackish and flaking tulip bulb, or (perhaps more exciting as far as I am concerned) those bigger bulbs from warmer countries which need pot cultivation here – species of South American *Hippeastrum*, perhaps, or their relative the *Phaedranassa*; vividly flowered *Haemanthus* from South Africa, or poisonous *Boöphone* with its fan of narrow leaves almost as decorative as its flattish red flower-head.

In seeds and bulbs there resides without doubt the pulse of life which gives gardening much of its magic. It is there too in the seasonal growth of plants in which as temperate gardeners we are privileged to assist, something one might miss in the tropics, where plants often obey no seasonal changes.

The British are often accused of being plantsmen rather than garden designers. I have wondered if a probably unsuspected interest in being constantly involved in plant growth is not as much part of this attitude as the more obvious desire to enjoy as many diverse plant forms as possible. This desire renders many of our gardens informal, even wilderness-like, in such strong contrast to the permanently laid-down framework of the formal French or Italian garden which needs constant attention with the shears to keep it perfect.

The shears are a restrictive practice which in a way deny the pulse of life. Our informal gardens certainly change relatively fast, often outgrow themselves and may eventually need the most drastic treatment, in contrast to the calm sophistication of a great Italian formal garden which – all stonework, hedges and topiary – can persist for centuries. The Italian designers created these as a frame for living, while the informal layout, whether a cottage plot or the acres of a Savill Garden, provides life itself, even if it eventually destroys itself. Maybe, as Sir Frederick Gibberd wrote in a 1979 article, 'the impermanence of garden design is one of its attractions'.

Perhaps most people regard the annual production of flowers as the most important function of their plants whatever they may be, but there are other, more subtle pleasures in the seasonal development of plants. Going back to the seed, one might admire the way so many plants make sure the delicate first leaves are least affected by being dragged out of the soil into the light, by the way the seedling stem is crooked to form a relatively strong 'elbow' which pushes up first and then hauls up the leafy end. Bulbs very often protect their flower buds in similar ways. E.A. Bowles noted this, for example, of crocuses: 'the two leaves are tightly bound round by a sheathing leaf so that their tips are pressed together to form a sharp point that cleaves the ground and makes way for the fragile flower, in much the same way that you put your two hands together and hold them in front of your head when diving into the water . . .'.

Crocuses can in this way thrust through gravel or asphalt; I have seen daffodils force their way through 8 cm. of tarmac, and tree shoots and roots can do much better. In Corfu I recall a huge stone block riven in half by a stone pine which must, many decades back, have germinated in some small fissure on its top. Perhaps the most remarkable example of plant power I have seen was the lifting of a large concrete paving slab by a single horse mushroom. This apparent miracle occurs because the mushroom's fragile individual cells swell inexorably as they take up water at the time destined for the development of the fruiting body, for that is what a mushroom is.

But let us return to leaves, many of which emerge from their buds in the most delicate manner. Observe those of beech trees, first deeply folded, shaking themselves out as the woods take on that special 'young' green that marks spring in many parts of Britain. The garden alchemilla is well called lady's mantle, for it unfolds like a pleated skirt. It is amazing to see the leaves of rhubarb, large and strong, barely two or three days after they seemed to be hard knobs, literally crumpled into a tight ball. One of the most astonishing openings is that of the multi-lobed leaf of the Monarch of the East or *Sauromatum guttatum*. One segment unrolls from the first, four more from this pair, and so on in what looks like a conjurer's trick with a rolled-up newspaper (better than the performance of its long, thin, briefly evil-smelling flower, which eventually collapses at the base like a caliph after an orgy). Or take the tulip tree, *Liriodendron tulipifera*, where a succession of leaves arises from one point, each beginning in a large oval stipule sheath which drops off when the young leaf is fully developed, to reveal the next embryo leaf in a tiny sheath, and so *ad-infinitum* like a Chinese puzzle.

There is a similar minor magic in the sudden transformation of the pale brown knobs of roseroot, *Sedum roseum*, to rosetted pale green leaf ruffs with the pink centres which will be the flowers, while I always feel that the development of the related 'ice plants' – *Sedum spectabile* and its kind – is a pleasure to watch throughout its seven- or eight-month progress from the first signs of the young blue-green foliage. There is a handful of plants which give this full season of pleasure, unlike many perennials which simply become coarse. Even the knobbly roots of Solomon's seal (*Polygonatum*) seem full of promise before they push up their greyish stems, unfurl their foliage and eventually dangle their row of little white bells and finally, perhaps, round berries. Perhaps the best of all are the ferns, from the time we can discern the furred leaves breaking from their root ball, where they have huddled all winter like a hibernating hedgehog, to uncurl upwards through a crozier stage – royal fern is specially good at this – to full deployment of the frond.

Flower buds give similar pleasure to the observant. I recall being delighted as a child by the little dunces' caps of California poppy (*Eschscholzia*) pushed off as the gay flowers expand; while the way a crumpled new-emerged poppy flower straightens its thin petals is reminiscent of a butterfly emerging from its chrysalis and stiffening its wings in the air. Think too of the perfection that develops from the bud of a hybrid tea rose, or of those giant tuberous begonias whose huge flowers sometimes look more like tissue-paper confections than anything natural.

Germination and new growth arising, leaves unfurling, flowers 'blowing' – to use the old poetic term – are part of the seasonal cycle in the garden. It is a cycle in which the gardener must be constantly alert: to deadhead plants which have bloomed or to remove early-flowering annuals bodily; to control the often rank growth of later summer, and trim back the dying leaves and stems in autumn: throughout he has the power to manipulate his garden so that its effect at a given time is as good as it can be. And of course seasonal change gives him an infinity of permutations in his initial planning, which needs a lot of care if plantings are to have enough colours, let alone attractive associations, throughout the season. Some gardeners with plenty of time still plan ahead in such detail that they can carry out replacement of one set of plants, once over, with ready-to-flower specimens of another carefully grown on in frames or reserve beds; but few of us have the space to do this, nor maybe the inclination. This is perhaps why grey, silver and other foliage plants have become so popular, for their use among flowering plants bridges the gaps in timing and helps to conceal the ugliness of many plants once they have bloomed.

The vagaries of our climate may in any case play havoc with the most careful schemes based on averages. But we can always be fairly sure that, though an early season will give spaced-out flowers from perhaps the beginning of March, and in a later one many shrubs and bulbs may not get going properly till May, everything will even out more or less by early summer, and then it is a matter of how early the first frosts come which controls the ending of the basic gardening season, especially if it relies to any extent on tender summer flowers. But all season long our garden plants go through various stages of growth and steady expansion.

Behind all this visible growth lie complicated engineering systems that the gardener seldom considers. The flimsy flowers mentioned earlier have to become strong enough to maintain their display and insect-attracting

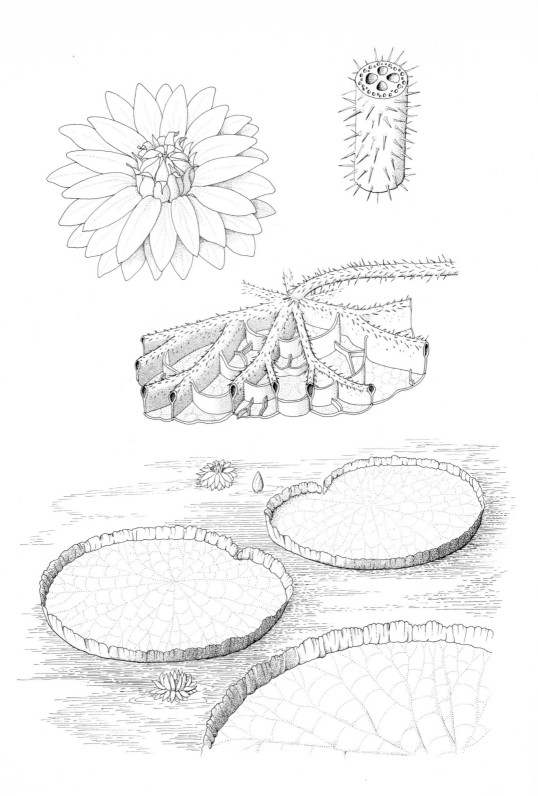

Victoria amazonica

capacities for a few days, though some produce incredible beauty for a few hours only, like the tigridia, passionflower or huge night-blooming cereus, a profligacy of perfection.

Likewise even the frailest annual has to have stems capable of withstanding wind and rain. If you handle a sunflower stem it seems not particularly strong, but they can grow 3 or 4 metres high with no trouble at all, while the record height is over 6 m. Such erect structures have internal 'girders' in the form of vascular bundles, and sections of their stems are reminiscent of architects' drawings of high ferro-concrete buildings. In the case of palms, their structure is more like that of a geodetic design.

The veins of leaves are reinforcement too, keeping them, in the main, flat-surfaced and fairly rigid though they are so thin. They are the solar panels which give life to the plant. Some leaves are of truly astonishing dimensions. There are giant aroids with paddle-shaped leaves three times the height of a man, but the biggest leaf recorded is that of a palm, *Raphia taedigera*, whose stalk alone is 5 m long and carries a 'blade' up to 22 m long carrying leaflets to a breadth of 12 m – a single leaf far bigger than many a town garden today!

However, the supreme example of leaf structure in engineering terms remains, I feel, that of the giant waterlily, *Victoria amazonica*. Though only 2 m across, a leaf is strong enough to support an average man, for on the under-side there are thick, radiating, tubular ribs and a series of thinner cross-ribs. It was this structure which gave Sir Joseph Paxton the idea for the curving, hollow metal framing of the Crystal Palace, as he freely admitted, writing 'Nature was the engineer – nature has provided the leaf with horizontal and transverse girders and supports that I, borrowing from it, have adapted in this building'.

This may seem an example of a permanent fabric rather than of the pulse of life; but in cultivation, as at Kew, the *Victoria* is usually grown as an annual, its leaves spreading by up to half a square metre every day in the early stages.

One eminent botanist, Professor G.E. Fogg, has written that 'although most people will feel fairly sure of what they understand by the word, "growth" has little precise meaning in the strictly scientific sense'. Perhaps we need do no more than recognize growth as the continuing pulse of life which is, with plants as indeed with all living organisms, what 'makes them tick'.

In a fully natural environment plants and other life-forms tick together in a kind of brutal harmony – brutal because there is such a welter of waste and over-production; so many billions of pollen grains, millions of seeds needed that one tree may grow; so much competition and endless death and decay, the cycle completed back to its elements, as one can see most clearly in a tropical rain-forest. In the very unnatural environment of our gardens we try and avoid such waste and loss, and we gain a different knowledge of plants from that of the ecologist. As we increase this knowledge our appreciation of their behaviour in the artificial garden situation improves. We learn how to improve their growth by feeding and training, how to extend flowering seasons and otherwise control growth by deadheading, cutting back or more specific pruning, and begin to react instinctively to plants suffering from lack of water, underfeeding or pest and disease attack. Human beings suffer from similar problems; plants may not have such complex life systems as ourselves but they are by no means simple, and in some circumstances the reasons for their success or failure are by no means always obvious.

The better our knowledge of our plants' internal processes and reactions, even if it is instinctive rather than scientifically-based, the better gardeners we become and, I believe, our pleasure in plants is enhanced – and that, surely, is what gardening is about. Maybe having 'green fingers' is really a deep understanding of the pulse of life in the green world.

Propagation

Roy Hay, M.B.E., V.M.H.

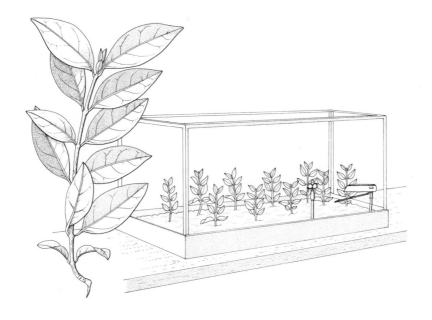

M Y FIRST choice of the aspect of gardening that had intrigued me most was plant breeding, because I spent the first ten years of my working life in the wholesale seed trade, mainly on the breeding and selecting of flowers. But on reflection I decided that propagation had given me more interest and satisfaction than any other horticultural activity. Looking back I think this fascination stemmed from exciting years when I was a schoolboy in the 1920s, when my father was superintendent of London's central Royal parks. When I was fourteen he wrote to my headmaster and said it was time my proper education began and that I would not be attending school the following Tuesday because he was taking me to the Chelsea Flower Show. Years afterwards the headmaster told me he was so flabbergasted that he agreed that I would have the day off! Since then I have attended every Chelsea Flower Show.

That was the period when my father and Lord Wigram, the private secretary to King George V, persuaded His Majesty that there were many beautiful wild flowers in Nepal and Kashmir awaiting introduction and he wrote to the Maharajahs of these states asking them to collect and send seeds here.

I can still feel the wild excitement as the batches of dried specimens and seeds arrived and even more excitement when George Taylor, now Sir George Taylor, who was then a botanist at the British Museum, South Kensington, discovered among them new species, even some new genera. Then there was the anxious waiting to see if the seeds would germinate and the joy when, for example, the first seedlings of *Meconopsis regia* and *M. dhwojii* first peeped through the soil.

I remember the great day when a consignment of plants of *Primula sonchifolia* arrived from Burma at London docks. They were great fat dormant buds, dug out of the frozen ground on the Hpmaw pass and sent home still frozen in the ship's cold store.

These and hundreds of other plants Father was instrumental in introducing, or re-introducing with the help of government friends or friends of friends overseas. Propagation once he had grown them was always an anxious problem. Would they set seeds here? Would they ripen and be viable? Could they be rooted from cuttings? – and so on.

The tricks we tried! Some seeds, I forget which, only germinate after a forest fire in their native land. So Father sowed them and burned a heap of straw over them. They germinated. Try as he might he could not root cuttings of *Cytisus battandieri*, that lovely small tree with the masses of upright golden 'candles' along its branches, which comes from the Atlas mountains of Morocco. He did not, of course, have the advantage of mist propagation in his day. If he had he would have been able to root a fair percentage of *Cytisus battandieri* cuttings. He did root some, however, by a very ingenious trick which I have never seen tried elsewhere and which one day I will find time to try myself. He took some fairly woody shoots of the cytisus and bored a small hole through them an inch or so from the base. He then threaded through the hole a small bundle of thin roots of the tree, some 3 in. long. Most of the cuttings took root and produced fine plants. A curious phenomenon, for which I have never seen any convincing explanation, is that when, say, camellia cuttings are tied in a bundle of a dozen or more they root more quickly and consistently than if they are set out to root singly, either with mist or not.

But there are so many tricks to learn about propagation. We have many new aids: growth-promoting hormones laced with a fungicide such as captan to minimize the risk of rotting; mist propagation, which not only hastens root formation but enables us to root cuttings that we could never have rooted before; and anti-desiccant compounds, which we spray on the leaves and which again hasten rooting by reducing transpiration and so minimize losses – all these are valuable aids. More about these later. But they do not replace the experience that the skilled propagator must acquire the hard way, by trial and error, patiently learning and remembering the right stage of growth, time of year, size of cutting, choice of rooting medium and many other factors that spell success or failure.

I think the 'green fingers' idea is a lot of nonsense. You seldom hear anybody saying that a young son or nephew has green fingers – it is always an old aunt, mother or, even more likely, an old grandma. And in spite of some dubious researchers claiming that some people have magical vibrations or something that they can transmit when handling plants, I think grandma's success with plants was due to her long experience, her powers of observation and her ability to remember what she did last time when things went well or when they went wrong and to act accordingly. Take one example – that lovely little shrub that covers itself in golden blossom at the end of June, *Genista lydia*. It is not easy to root cuttings of it, but easier if you have a mist propagation bench. But even so you have to catch the young shoots just right. Take them when they are too soft, and they will rot. Take them, say, a week or two later and they will root in three weeks. Leave them another two or three weeks to become a little too hard and they may take three months to root, if indeed they ever do.

With plants, especially shrubs, that you have found difficult to root it is worthwhile taking and inserting a few cuttings once a week over a period of, say, four weeks and noting which batch rooted best.

Even if we have a good memory – and as we grow older our memories play us tricks and seem to be full of blank spaces – it does pay to keep a diary and note in it dates when we sowed seeds or took cuttings, divided plants or planted bulbs. I have always considered that the most valuable books in a gardener's library are the diaries he has kept over the years.

Let us return to the various aids to propagation, and here I am thinking about raising seeds and rooting cuttings. Mist propagation I have already mentioned and I think it is the greatest single breakthrough we have seen regarding cutting rooting.

There is equipment for large-scale propagation but there are also small kits suitable for use in an ordinary amateur's greenhouse and many hundreds of cuttings may be rooted over a few months in these small units. Not only do many cuttings root more quickly and with a higher percentage of successes than by ordinary means, but we can often root much larger cuttings. For example, quite large shoots of heathers with a small head of side growths will root under mist and produce a plant as large as you would buy in a nursery in a matter of weeks.

Then a small mist unit is a splendid place to set seeds of primulas and polyanthus to germinate. You sow them, put them under the mist and forget them. If the seeds are viable, they come up like mustard and cress.

A trick known to few amateurs, and come to that not to all professionals, is the treatment of cuttings intended for rooting under mist with an anti-desiccant compound such as S.600, which we use to spray on Christmas trees to prevent the needles from dropping all over the carpet.

Nature is full of surprises. The idea behind rooting cuttings in a soil-warmed bed under mist is simply to prevent them from drying out and shrivelling through the transpiration of the moisture in their leaves. When you take a cutting and stick it in a pot of compost, it becomes a slowly dying piece of vegetation. It is a question of whether it dies before it can make enough roots to keep it alive. In a mist unit, a sensor switches on the mist when the moisture on the leaves of the cuttings dries off. In theory, if the cuttings are always covered with a film of moisture they will not wilt and will be vigorous pieces of vegetation capable of being kept in full light and will quickly root.

One would think that the layer of moisture would be all that is necessary. But my gardener Michael Lewis found some years ago that by spraying cuttings with S.600 before switching on the mist, and giving them another spraying two days later, rooting was greatly accelerated, especially with conifers. I have used anti-desiccants even without mist with considerable success to help cuttings to root.

We live in an age when almost everything seems to be made of plastic, from sausage skins to footwear. But plastic film can help us enormously with our problems of propagation. Cuttings inserted in a pot of a suitable rooting medium, watered and covered with a plastic bag tied tightly around the rim of the pot will often root easily and will not need watering until they are ready to be removed and potted. This is the same principle as the old Wardian case. The moisture which is given off, condenses on the plastic and runs down into the soil again and so is not lost.

We now have even more sophisticated and efficient propagating 'domes'. The 'Seal and Grow' is an ingenious piece of equipment. It consists of two plastic rings very similar to the wooden rings the ladies use into which they can clip a piece of embroidery or tapestry on which they are working. In this case a plastic 'dome' is clipped to cover a batch of cuttings or pots of seeds.

This is then blown up and plugged with a small plastic plug. Again, if the rooting or seed-sowing medium is moistened correctly, the plastic dome is not removed until the cuttings or seedlings are ready for potting or pricking off.

While not strictly part of the propagation process, I suppose I can include the use of plastic pots as the next stage in a plant's life after we have succeeded in starting it off in life with a good set of roots.

Being a thrifty Scot, I hesitate to give away all my clay pots and replace them with plastic pots. But I know I should and I will over the foreseeable future, for several reasons. First, I find most plants – indeed all that we grow – are happier in plastic pots than in clay. The plastic pots do not dry out as fast as the clay pots because the moisture does not evaporate through the side of the pot. Thus the soil temperature is usually warmer because there is less cooling through the effect of evaporation as occurs with clay pots. Also, plants in plastic pots do not need watering so often as those in clay pots, for the same reason.

Furthermore, plastic pots are much more adapted for the modern method of automatic watering – sub-irrigation, because they have many holes in the base through which water can rise by capillary attraction to keep the soil in the pot moist. With clay pots one usually has to go to the trouble of putting a wick of some kind through the hole in the bottom to take up the water from the moist bench. And here again plastic comes into its own. Sub-irrigation benches in a greenhouse are covered with sand, or nowadays quite often with plastic matting of some kind. This is kept moist by various methods, semi- or fully automatic and the plants in their plastic pots sitting on this moist plastic bed draw up water as and when they require it.

Plastics, like so many other modern inventions, are wonderful in their place. But I would ask every reader of these pages to eschew plastic flowers and indeed to go out and wage war against them. We have a supply of small cards saying 'Plastic flowers lower the tone of this establishment' and I and many others hand these in with the bill or place them around under plastic arrangements whenever we see them in expensive hotels and restaurants.

Let plastics be our servants and not our masters.

To sum up, my advice to anyone who thinks that propagation is too daunting to try, is to have a go. Start with cuttings of easy plants like ivy, geraniums or fuchsias. With a few successes you will be encouraged to try all kinds of plants and you will be surprised how successful you will be.

Some Thoughts on Designing a Garden

P.S. Stagg, N.D.H.

G ARDEN design is the power to see and give form to beautiful things. The work of the true artist has great regard for nature and this rule is paramount. Flowers look even more beautiful when growing in a natural and harmonious setting. A landscape gardener's skill relies wholly on a wide knowledge of trees, shrubs and plants in general. Without these basic tools of the trade, expensive and disappointing mistakes will be made. A landscape architect, a term of French origin, thinks generally in terms of stone and brick with a limited knowledge of plants. Fine English gardens such as Stourhead and Sheffield Park, to name but two, are excellent examples of a landscape gardener's work.

In considering a design, the plants and trees become the paint on the canvas and it is quite inconceivable that an attempt should be made by a non-plantsman. The main factors to consider in designing a garden are:

(a) Size and shape of the site
(b) Formal or informal layout
(c) Type of soil: clay, sandy or chalky
(d) Location: seaside, rural or industrial
(e) Aspect: shady, sunny, frost pocket, windy, exposed.

These factors will determine the choice of plants and type of garden. Good design must be approached with foresight. What will the effect be after ten to twenty years' growth? Although a small garden is more difficult to design than a larger one, the same principles apply, the prime laws are simplicity and restraint.

It is useless to try and develop a rhododendron and camellia garden on a chalky soil, or to plant trees which are susceptible to wind blow, e.g. *Acer saccharinum* or *Robinia pseudoacacia*, on a wind-swept site without first establishing wind breaks: these could include trees such as evergreen oak (*Quercus ilex*), Austrian pine (*Pinus nigra*), *Cupressocyparis leylandii* and sycamore, and among shrubs, *Hippophae rhamnoides*, *Euonymus fortunei*, *Pyracantha atalantioides*, *Elaeagnus commutata* and *Tamarix gallica*.

In devising an original design, the site should be viewed from all directions. How will the front and back garden look from the house? How will the house look from the front gate?

If sheds or glasshouses are wanted, group these together at the bottom of the garden and screen with a hedge or large shrub border. Alternatively, a shed could be of an attractive design taking the form of a summerhouse and become a focal point of the garden.

Competition for the sun is the first guide in formulating your design. Place the main borders or beds facing south and put paths if required, although these are best avoided unless they are of grass, on the side that faces north or east. Always avoid cluttering up the middle or the foreground of the site with small beds or individual trees or shrubs.

Preferably the foreground should consist of a large expanse of grass with a background of trees and shrubs skilfully placed to give an illusion of distance.

Screen unsightly views and try to achieve an attractive skyline. Whilst both sides of the garden should not be the same, balance should be the objective; for example, if three trees are growing on one side of the garden, offset this major focal point by planting one tree on the other side. Avoid planting forest-type trees in a small garden, as they will eventually outgrow their positions. Try to achieve a harmonious effect by planting associated plants, e.g. dwarf conifers with heathers and azaleas, climbing roses with clematis. Establish good hedges to segregate formal gardens from the informal part. Boundaries should be planted to give privacy and shelter, particularly from the colder quarters, and should be given priority in the design.

Contrast of design is also very important; a rose garden, heather garden, bog garden, or rock garden leading from a spacious lawn is effective, especially if perspective is applied again to give the illusion of distance. Grass paths converging slightly or curving and disappearing around a shrub border are subtle ways of achieving this.

Formal gardens generally consist in their design of straight lines or

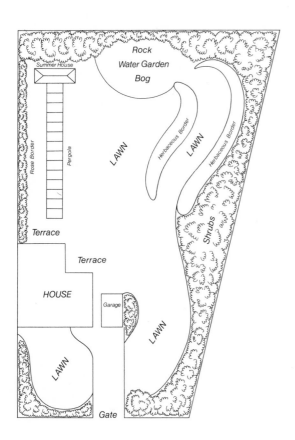
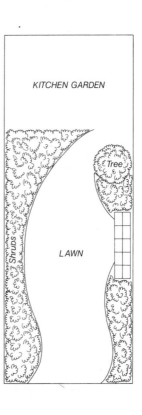

geometrical curves; rose gardens and knot gardens are good examples. Most garden lovers have their own particular tastes and many prefer informal layouts of woodland glades, rock gardens and gracefully curved shrub borders. In these circumstances, try to lay out the lines of borders and paths flowing one way. Others prefer formal gardens of roses or irises; here care must be taken to avoid flatness by planting erect Irish yews or junipers or pillar roses at certain focal points. When planting beds or borders, be bold and ensure they are of a good width. Later, make sure the chosen shrubs or perennials are in reasonably large groups. This rule applies equally to herbaceous borders, shrub borders and heather gardens.

Before firm ideas begin to form, it is prudent to consider features which may become focal points or become dominant in the overall design, e.g. garden seat, arbour, fountain, summerhouse, pergola or pool. The siting of a focal point is the first consideration on which the design is formed.

As previously mentioned, the foreground should be open with a large expanse of grass. In a small town garden, this may be replaced by stone, gravel or brick but, in all situations, the background should consist of trees and shrubs of which at least a third should be evergreen to give depth and winter interest. The background may be a hedge, but deep shrub borders of carefully selected shrubs will give far more year-round interest, particularly if underplanted with spring- and autumn-flowering bulbs.

If a hedge is required, it could be a formal clipped type of yew, holly, beech or *Thuja plicata*, or alternatively, an informal type of *Cotoneaster simonii* or *C. lactea*, shrub rose or *Forsythia*, to mention but a few.

In my view, paths generally should be avoided, but if unavoidable, placed towards the shady side of the garden. They can of course be enhanced by a pergola and become a very attractive feature or part of a rose garden leading to an arbour. A terrace or patio is an ideal way of linking the house to the garden. The house should always be an integral part of the garden. Walls were invented to support books on the inside and plants on the outside. If the terrace or patio has ground rising up from it, a retaining wall or dry wall will be necessary; the top of this can be planted with procumbent shrubs, forming an interesting and attractive border. Where the land slopes sharply away, further terraces may be desirable; the basic rule is that the horizontals are wider and the verticals shorter with each successive lower terrace. This will give a pleasing concave effect.

A loggia is a terrace with overhead timbers attached to the house, and this is a splendid way of supporting a wide range of climbing plants and integrating the house and garden. A water feature on the patio or terrace is also most attractive but should be carefully sited: whilst the use of water gives added interest, it should always be in the sunlight and not overhung by trees. In the vicinity of the house, a formal pool, rectangular, square or circular in shape with a small fountain, creates a distinct style, particularly fascinating if stocked with fish and aquatic plants. Water spouting from the face of a wall

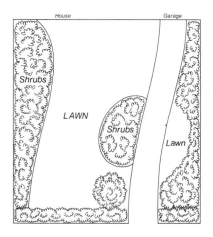

and falling into a semicircular basin provides a relaxing sound and obviously enhances a patio or terrace.

If the garden has a stream or river passing through it, this may form the major feature in an informal garden. It could effectively be linked to a bog garden which, planted with primulas, is a delight to see. Water can be associated with a rock garden and there are immense possibilities on a sloping site with waterfalls and small pools. Badly constructed concrete pools crack and leak and are always difficult to repair. However, Butyl sheeting is an excellent modern material admirably suited to the construction of pools of considerable size and shape; a waterfall, if required, can quite simply be incorporated by placing the sheeting behind the stone forming the shelf up into the pool above. Water lilies and other aquatics, together with marginal plants, add colour interest to any garden.

Recommended marginal plants for pools:
Acorus calamus 'Variegatus', *Caltha palustris* 'Plena', *Butomus umbellatus*, *Iris kaempferi*, *Mimulus luteus*, *Lyschitum americanum*, *Osmunda regalis*, *Pontederia cordata*, *Scirpus tabernaemontani* 'Zebrinus', and *Typha minima*.
Aquatics:
Aponogeton distachyus, *Eichhornia crassipes* 'Major', *Stratiotes aloides*, *Nymphaea marliacea* 'Rosea', *N.* James Brydon', *N. pygmaea* 'Helvola', and *N. pygmaea* 'Rubra'.

If a rock garden is required, one large stone is more effective than ten or twenty smaller ones. The courses of stone should give a feeling of conforming to lines of stratification. The stone should be laid so that it appears to come out of the ground naturally, and the rock should be in strata to make one impressive outcrop. Peg the area out in three rectangles, the largest at the rear. Keep primary and secondary joints clear of stone and use these joints for planting. Recesses and gulleys can be formed by leaving out stone or using smaller stones where appropriate.

Having established the main focal points, the importance of planting and ultimate effect is paramount. Select key trees and shrubs carefully, plant the shrubs in groups of three or five, infill these with shrubs which will inevitably be removed as the key shrubs develop. Between 30% and 50% of the key trees and shrubs should be evergreens, so important during the winter months. Careful choices will give double pleasure, e.g. spring flowers and fine evergreen foliage (*Camellia japonica* 'Jupiter'), or good spring flowers with excellent autumn foliage (*Amelanchier canadensis* or an allied species).

Trees will effectively break the skyline, and screen unsightly views with a variety of shapes. Form, scent and colour should be the aim. I think the following do well in average conditions:

Betula jacquemontii, B. pendula 'Dalecarlica', *Acer griseum, A. nikoense, Catalpa bignonioides* 'Aurea', *Cytisus battandieri, Davidia involucrata, Gleditsia triacanthos* 'Sunburst', *Magnolia kobus, M. × soulangiana* 'Picture', *Malus* 'Golden Hornet', *M.* 'John Downie', *Prunus subhirtella* 'Autumnalis Rosea' and

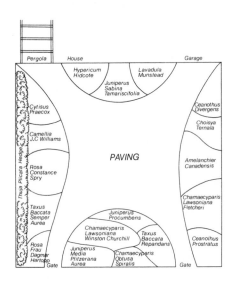

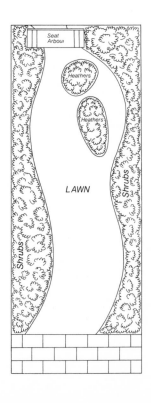

'Pendula Rubra', *Pyrus salicifolia* 'Pendula', *Robinia pseudoacacia* 'Frisia', *Sorbus sargentiana* and *Cercis siliquastrum*.

Conifers
Chamaecyparis lawsoniana 'Winston Churchill', *Cryptomeria japonica* 'Elegans', *Juniperus chinensis, Libocedrus decurrens, Metasequoia glyptostroboides, Pinus mugo, Taxus baccata* 'Elegantissima' and 'Fastigiata'.

A few recommended shrubs
Acer palmatum 'Dissectum', *Aesculus parviflora, Amelanchier canadensis, Berberis darwinii*, camellias in variety, *Ceanothus divergens*, C. *gloriosus*, C. 'Cascade', *Choisya ternata, Cistus laurifolius, Cornus mas, Corylopsis willmottiae*, cotoneasters in variety, *Cytisus battandieri*, C. × *beanii*, C. × *praecox, Elaeagnus pungens* 'Maculata', *Erica* in variety, *Fuchsia* 'Mrs. Popple', *Genista aetnensis*, G. *tinctoria* 'Royal Gold', *Hamamelis* in variety, *Hibiscus syriacus* 'Blue Bird', *Hydrangea sargentiana, Hypericum* in variety, *Kolkwitzia amabilis*, magnolias in variety, *Mahonia bealei*, M. × 'Charity', M. *japonica, Myrtus communis, Osmanthus delavayi, Parrotia persica, Pernettya mucronata* 'Davis's Hybrids', *Philadelphus* 'Beauclerk', P. 'Belle Etoile', P. 'Virginal', *Pieris formosa* 'Wakehurst', *Poncirus trifoliata, Pyracantha* 'Mojave', rhododendrons (including azaleas) in variety, *Rhus cotinus* 'Foliis Purpureis', *Romneya coulteri* and hybrids, *Rosa xanthina* 'Canary Bird', R. 'Constance Spry', R. 'Frühlingsgold', R. 'Frühlingsmorgen', R. 'Nevada', R. *rugosa* 'Frau Dagmar Hastrup', *Rubus deliciosus, Syringa* × *prestoniae*, S. × *josiflexa* 'Bellicent', S. *microphylla* 'Superba', and *Viburnum* in variety.

Bamboos
Arundinaria nitida, A. *murieliae, Chusquea couleou*, and *Phyllostachys viridi-glaucescens*.

Front gardens are often dominated by a drive to the garage, usually straight from the garage to the front gate. The majority of people want as much privacy from their neighbours as possible and achieve this by planting hedges and shrub borders. A curved drive carefully planted with shrubs will effectively screen the gap which straight drives make (see drawings). It also sets the following lines which, if repeated when forming shrub borders, will ensure complete harmony in the overall design. As previously mentioned, paths, if unavoidable, can be immeasurably improved by pergolas. Avoid placing a pergola in the centre, dividing the garden into two. Ideally it should be placed on one side (see drawing), leading to an arbour constructed in similar material. A heavy structure of brick or stone pillars with timber beams is aesthetically more acceptable than a light wooden structure; furthermore, it is stout enough to support heavy climbing plants. The climbing plants I particularly favour include:

Actinidia chinensis, A. *kolomikta, Campsis grandiflora, Clematis macropetala* and

C.m. 'Markham's Pink', *C. montana grandiflora*, *C.* 'Mrs. Cholmondely', *Hedera helix* 'Gold Heart', *Lonicera periclymenum* 'Belgica', *Lonicera* × *tellmanniana*, *Rosa* 'Handel' and 'Golden Showers' and *Vitis coignetiae*.

Although herbaceous borders have lost some of their appeal because of the work involved in maintaining them, an old-fashioned or traditional border is a delightful feature bringing bold splashes of colour and giving an opportunity of creating vistas linking one part of the garden to another or highlighting a feature at the end of the vista. Borders also provide a wonderful supply of flowers for the house.

Herbaceous borders, single or double, should follow the main axial line from the house. Borders should run down the garden and not across it, and they should be wide enough to give a feeling of depth (about 12 ft or more is ideal). They can be backed by hedges, shrubs or walls, arranged in straight lines or curves, and may be planned to give colour over a long period or, as I prefer, to flower about the same time in midsummer.

Borders confined to specific colour shades of blue and grey, yellow and red, or white and grey are impressive. In any event, when planning the border, harmonize colours by placing the strong dark blues or purples towards the ends and pastel shades in the centre; combinations of colours such as pink and grey, blue and yellow, white and yellow, are particularly effective. I would include the following plants in any border:
Achillea filipendulina 'Coronation Gold', *Aconitum* 'Bressingham Spire', *Aruncus sylvester* (*dioicus*), *Baptisia australis*, *Campanula lactiflora* 'Prichards Variety', *Clematis recta* 'Grandiflora', *Crinum* × *powellii*, *Echinops ritro*, *Geranium ibericum* (of gardens = *G.* × *magnificum*), *Gypsophila paniculata* 'Bristol Fairy', *Hemerocallis* in variety, *Hosta* in variety, *Kirengeshoma palmata*, *Liatris callilepis*, *Monarda* 'Cambridge Scarlet', *Oenothera* 'Fireworks', *Phlox decussata* and *paniculata* in variety, *Polygonum amplexicaule* 'Atrosanguineum', *Salvia haematodes*, *S. superba*, *Sidalcea* 'Loveliness' and 'Rose Queen', *Solidago* 'Cloth of Gold', and *Veronica gentianoides*.

In conclusion, those unfortunate enough not to have a garden should take note of the remarkable results achieved with window boxes and tubs. Very small town gardens, often paved to accommodate cars, are obviously ideal for this type of treatment. A few climbing plants and shrubs can soften boundary brick walls; the inclusion of just one small to medium-sized tree, if space permits, would complete the layout and improve the street enormously.

Of Chalk,
Flints
and Peat

Kenneth A. Beckett

HAVING an 'affinity with' or a 'feeling for' the soil may sound rustically romantic, but I am convinced that all good gardeners have it, whether they admit it or not. This feeling or affinity can only be acquired by those who are intimately concerned with their plants, particularly in getting to know their essential requirements. Some plants grow superlatively well in one soil, but transfer them to another and they languish or fail to thrive whatever we do. It may be a matter of drainage, which in turn is tied up with texture and humus content. It may be that the soil is too limy or too acid or that a certain essential plant food or trace element is missing. This essential aspect of gardening is heightened if we have an itinerant streak and move to houses and pastures new from time to time. Getting to know what will or will not grow in one soil is, I feel, half the joy of gardening. There is also no doubt in my mind that the experiences of the first plot of soil we dig and plant can colour our approach and preferences in gardening for the rest of our lives.

I count myself fortunate to have become fascinated by plants at a very early age and to have started gardening on the chalk downs of Sussex. For more than a dozen years the thin, whitish, flinty soil, dry in summer, surprisingly sticky in a wet winter, was the only soil I knew. Several lessons were quickly learnt: 4-6 in. of soil over pure chalk cannot be deeply dug, and humus is the key to soil fertility. When about eight years of age I was given a small scruffy tomato plant and was told I should put plenty of manure around it. Sheep then grazed the downland turf just beyond the end of our garden and I quickly collected a bucketful of manure and poured it around the tomato. I can clearly remember my astonishment at the speed and size that the plant grew in so short a time afterwards, A real 'Jack and the Beanstalk' performance which confirmed my faith in manure for all time.

Growing vegetables and then bedding plants and quick-growing colourful hardy annuals was fun and presented no difficulties with adequate manure and moisture. It was my first great gardening love, rock and alpine plants, which really made me aware of the soil. Many of my favourites, in particular most of the bell flowers, saxifrages, thymes, pinks (*Dianthus*), many small bulbs etc. throve splendidly, others did not. Soon I wanted to try summer-flowering heaths and heathers and dwarf rhododendrons and had to use pots of peaty compost to enjoy their charms. Soon also I wanted to make a small rock garden, and this made me conscious of the bedrock beneath the soil layer. Chalk lumps are useless for building a rock garden. Their soft crumbly nature has resulted in the smoothly eroded contours of the Downs covered by springy turf and a profusion of mainly small plants not unlike the alpines of higher country. Only in the occasional chalk pit does one gain any impression of a rock scenery. About this time I started roaming farther afield by bike and on one trip found myself in the sandstone country of mid-Sussex. The great sandstone boulder outcrops were a revelation and started a desire to see real mountains and their plant life. Little then did I realize that this love of mountains and mountain plants would lead me to the rugged vastnesses of the Sierra Nevada of California, the Southern Alps of New Zealand and the majestic Andes with its vast and terrifyingly desolate screes.

These early experiences taught me not to despise any rock when it comes to building a rock garden or similar home for small plants. The softer sandstones are frowned upon by the experts as building material, but if available should not be ignored. One of my most successful efforts had been the building of a low outcrop in carstone, a rusty sandstone charged with lime from an overlay of chalk, best seen in the cliffs of Hunstanton in Norfolk. On this outcrop *Ramonda* and *Haberlea* flourish in crevices, and the Andean *Azorella* forms a wide low cushion. Of some surprise has been the success of *Pratia angulata* rambling across a ledge of crushed carstone and forming a real mat of tiny jagged-toothed leaves spangled for months on end with small white hand-shaped flowers. Lime-loving saxifrages do well and particularly that queen of mountain pinks *Dianthus alpinus*. *Androsace primuloides* and *A. sempervivoides* seem to appreciate a ledge of carstone brash, as does the small mountain form of our native *Scabiosa columbaria*, generally listed in catalogues as '*S. alpina*'. Lime-loving ferns also appreciate this little outcrop and the native black spleenwort (*Asplenium adiantum-nigrum*) has settled down well. A particular surprise has been the success of *Coprosma brunnea*, a mat-forming New Zealand shrublet all too seldom seen in Britain. This was set out as seedlings two years ago and I look forward to the day when the wiry bronzy-leaved stems will be thickly spangled with semi-translucent blue-flecked opalescent fruits.

Flints are very much despised as an accompaniment for rock and alpine plants, and there is no doubt they are useless as building material for the traditional rock garden. Nevertheless I have a soft spot for the hard flint, for it invariably accompanies the chalk I grew up with. The chipped and broken flints that litter a chalk loam soil are not pretty, but a layer of them can form a permanent mulch not to be despised in conserving moisture and keeping the soil beneath cool. Light soils, both chalky and sandy, warm up rapidly in the summer and a high soil temperature down among the roots is not appreciated by many mountain plants. This is, I am sure, a cause of failure all too often overlooked. But I digress. Water-worn flints can have considerable aesthetic appeal and can form a splendid background for many plants. Just after the 1939-45 war the shingle beaches of Sussex – freed of trampling feet for five years – sported many seaside plants, among them sea beet (the progenitor of sugar beet) and sea rocket (*Cakile maritima*). It was not until some years later, though, that I viewed the vast stretch of Chesil Bank and its wonderful display of such showy wild flowers as sea poppy, thrift and sea campion. From then on down the years I have always had a niggling desire to create a shingle garden. Perhaps one day I will. Meanwhile chance has enabled me to create a substitute which I suspect is rather more rewarding and possibly unique.

When my wife and I took over a new garden a few years ago, every fussy little path was edged with serried ranks of water-worn flint boulders of

Cytisus x beanii

varying sizes. When moved and piled high they made an impressive sight – but what to do with them? Even before the last boulder was extracted and placed upon the pile, however, I knew. Mountain memories recalled boulder screes, some stark and almost without plants, others quickly vegetated and even wooded. I would try to create a boulder scree as a garden feature. Our flat garden did not present a suitable slope, so I adopted a stylized approach on the flat and created two boulder beds soon affectionately nicknamed Brighton and Hove. Luckily the soil was naturally sandy and well drained and in addition had once been an ash midden when the house was heated by solid fuel. Had this not been so, I should have felt obliged to fork in sand and/or gravel to make sure drainage was perfect. The two beds are contiguous, divided by a flagstone path and together curve for 30 ft around the side of an oval lawn. The boulders, some of them 1 ft (30 cm) or more across, were put in place fairly thickly, leaving plenty of cracks and larger gaps for plants. After planting, all bare soil was covered with very fine shingle. Several hundred plants now dwell among the boulders and some have thriven in a most satisfactory way. Indeed, a few things throve too well and started to take over less vigorous brethren. Surprisingly enough, one of these was the dainty little yellow alpine poppy, *Papaver kerneri*. Allowing it to seed the first year was a mistake. Subsequently seedlings came up thickly everywhere and had to be severely reduced. Obviously the fine shingle over sandy soil provided an ideal seed bed. The pretty little *Erinus alpinus*, sometimes likened to a very diminutive foxglove, is also spreading by its abundant seeds and will have to be watched. To provide some quick plant interest, rock roses, the lovely purple 'Delight' form of *Parahebe catarractae* and grey mats of *Alyssum wulfenianum* were allowed to grow unchecked, and this they did fast. Within two years the tide of their advancing stems had swallowed up attractively sculpted boulders and smaller choice plants alike. They had to go. Among choicer plants, several dwarf hardy geraniums have done well. Hard to beat is G. *dalmaticum*, forming low hummocks or mats of tiny lobed leaves above which are poised comparatively large blooms of clear rich pink. As a bonus some of the leaves turn crimson in autumn. *Geranium farreri* (often grown as G. *napuligerum*) has a tufted habit and stems that lie on the ground with upturned tips. The flowers are held vertically and range from palest pink to lilac or white. Much to my surprise it flowered in well under a year from seeds. Very much more robust by comparison is G. *traversii* with its flopping clumps and mats of decorative grey foliage and smallish wide open icing-pink blossoms. It is restricted in the wild to the tiny Chatham Islands in the South Pacific due east of Christchurch, New Zealand, but is surprisingly hardy. Several of the small hardy mountain hebes (shrubby veronicas) have done well among the boulders, noteworthy being H. *epacridea*, an uncommon mat-forming shrublet with crowded, thick-textured wavy leaves and terminal head-like clusters of small white flowers. Close by is the whipcord species H. *tetrasticha*, its dark green scale-like leaves arranged in four overlapping ranks on erect stems which soon branch and eventually form hummocks. Both these hebes failed to do well until transferred to the boulder beds, and I am sure the cool root run is the deciding factor.

Plants which spread moderately and neatly fill out cracks between closely set stones are a delight. Of particular appeal in this respect is *Potentilla eriocarpa*, a plant of the neatest disposition from the Himalaya. It has tiny, somewhat greyish strawberry leaves and a long succession of comparatively large cup-shaped yellow flowers. Already self-sown seedlings have appeared but I am sure that it will never rival the alpine poppy in profligacy. Several of the small St John's worts are thriving including the mat-forming *Hypericum repens*. Sadly the large and shapely bowl-shaped golden flowers always face downwards. Much more eye-catching is *H. trichocaulon*, a surprisingly hardy little plant from Crete. Its dense tufty mats are a picture when set with sealing-wax-red buds and yellow flowers. *H. polyphyllum* is probably the finest of the low-growing St John's worts but its woody-based hummocks can get quite large. Already my two-year plants from cuttings are 20 in. (50 cm) across, but I shall leave them for a year or so longer for the sake of their splendid showing of bright yellow blossoms.

To exploit to the full the soil and situation of his garden should be the dedicated aim of every true gardener. This of course means growing only those plants that like your conditions, but few gardeners are satisfied with such a situation. Soon, for example, we want to try impossibly tender plants in what we feel sure are sheltered or warm nooks, or feel a need to grow rhododendrons and their allies when we garden on chalk. Both activities have occupied me off and on for the past 30 years, but it was an interest in rhododendrons and ericas that led me to react against the chalk and seek comfort in peat. Looking back, it probably all started the first time I was taken to a heathland area in Surrey. A landscape of heather and pine trees with *Rhododendron ponticum* naturalized beneath was a revelation, so utterly different from my chalk downland birthplace. Added fascination was provided by peaty boggy hollows patterned with red and green sphagnum mosses and here and there a plant of sundew. Later, I paid my first visit to the R.H.S. Gardens at Wisley and roamed bewildered among the countless rhododendrons on Battleston Hill. Several years further on I became a student there and tried to get to grips with this great genus of some 800 species (plus many more hybrids and cultivars) but never really succeeded. The Heather Garden at Wisley also exerted a great appeal on me and I soon became a devotee of the heather allies *Daboecia, Phyllodoce, Menziesia, Cassiope, Andromeda, Gaultheria, Pernettya, Pieris*, etc. A trip to the Edinburgh Botanic Garden – the home of peat gardening – brought me face to face with the concept and possibilities of the peat bed. How curious that the compacted remains of sphagnum mosses or sedges in an arrested state of decay (for that is what peat is) should provide such a satisfying and successful medium for growing plants. Light, comparatively clean to handle and almost weed-free, it is the 'luxury soil' to use and plant in. It does provide cultural problems, however, as we shall see in due course. The first peat bed I made was on the boulder clay of Essex. Knowing the limy nature of the soil the bed was made about 1 ft (30 cm) deep and edged with a retaining wall of peat blocks. A mixture of moss and neutral sedge peat was used and proved successful. Although plants grew well, that first peat bed was fairly short-lived, for a year or so later it was carefully dismantled and brought to our present Norfolk garden. Here the soil is sandy and has a pH of 6.5, so is naturally acid enough to grow rhododendrons. With a soil base of this kind a peat layer of only 4 in. (10 cm) was deemed necessary and a larger bed constructed edged by a single thickness of peat blocks. All the plants settled in well and more were soon added. Three years later many plants have grown gratifyingly well, and as in the boulder bed some have over-excelled themselves.

Gaultheria procumbens, the creeping wintergreen of N. America, soon pushed out its slender far-creeping red rhizomes emitting at intervals tufts of glossy leaves, white urn-shaped flowers and, later, bright red berries. *G. cuneata* formed low glossy mounds, giving promise of the profuse white berries which are its star turn. The American form of the twin-flower, *Linnaea borealis americana*, crept flatly outwards with increasing vigour, and *Myrtus nummularia* has done likewise but more slowly. The latter plant is a prostrate evergreen shrublet formed of interlacing wiry stems set with pairs of tiny glossy deep green leaves and small white many-stamened flowers followed by pink berries. It grows on wettish heathland-like areas in southern South America. In such an area in Chile I once pitched my tent and just outside the entrance this plant grew. That same campsite also ties up with another of the early peat-bed plants, the southern hard fern, *Blechnum penna-marina*. This low-growing rhizomatous fern with its attractive reddish-bronzy flushed young fronds was dense and dominant and so thick below the nylon floor of the tent that it formed a tolerably comfortable mattress. Its denseness and vigour has been maintained in the peat bed and I feel that one day soon it will have to be curbed, despite my affection for it. This reminiscence touches upon a weakness of many gardeners – of which I am unashamedly one – to grow plants associated with places and people, sometimes even when they have no great garden merit.

While success has been considerable in the Norfolk peat bed – we are particularly proud of our flowering specimens of six different sorts of *Cassiope*, three of *Phyllodoce*, to say nothing of such uncommon species as *Tsusiophyllum* and *Andromeda polifolia macrophylla* – there have been troubles. Worst of these now are the weeds pearlwort and liverwort (*Marchantia*) which have insidiously invaded centres of small shrubs and mat-formers in such a way that they are difficult to extricate.

Associated with the true weeds are the introduced members which are behaving as such. Pretty *Pratia treadwellii* has gone on the rampage smothering all before it, while *Hydrocotyle moschata* – though too small to smother – infiltrates everything. I should have known better than to introduce the latter, but who would have guessed that *Ajuga pyramidalis* would behave as a weed? A tiny and treasured plant was popped in a vacant spot in the bed to add some variety of foliage and flower to the shrublets around. It soon proceeded to send out horizontal roots for yards around emitting tufts of leaves at intervals, then pressing on in the best colonizing way. It is now treated as a weed. One must be so careful of the unknown plant when it comes to peat gardening because once it becomes rampant major upheavals are required to remove it. Even so, the upheavals are not particularly traumatic. Peat is such a pleasure to handle and the refurbished area will give the excuse to purchase or scrounge some new plants.

The
Changing Face of
the Greenhouse
World

J.R.B. Evison, O.B.E., N.D.H., V.M.H.

I T IS A quaint quirk of human nature that the episodes one looks back on with affection in later years are not the good times but those when all was most difficult. Over 50 years ago I was thrown into the world of the greenhouse – and I say 'thrown' advisedly, for to my horror, within an hour of arriving for my first day's work I found myself placed in sole charge of a range of six greenhouses. They contained vines and peaches; it being November, all were dormant, so I had a little time to learn where the ventilator controls were and how to manage the valves on the cast-iron 4 in. hot-water pipes, which were the near-universal way of heating greenhouses then.

One grew up very quickly under such responsibility. Of course it was a matter of pride to go home and boast of having charge of four vineries and two peach houses; it was on that pride that the system worked, for having been so trusted, no youngster would allow anything to take priority over his charge; it also stimulated questions which provided a short cut to experience.

There was also the matter of fear. This was the end of the 1920s when there were some three million unemployed and the loss of a job a personal tragedy. This fear was embodied in the shape of the Head Gardener – the Old Man. In spite of the fact that many large estates were breaking up, he was still the autocratic chief of his little world, bowler-hatted as a badge of office and prone to wear a frock coat if there was any chance of a visitation by Higher Authority. He could and did sack on the spot for any offence he regarded as serious. Certainly impertinence or being late twice in a week would come into that category.

The Head Gardeners were a closely knit clan who knew each other well as friends or flower-show rivals. The gardens were largely staffed by journeymen – young men in training who in the interests of widening their experiences were rarely allowed to stay more than two years in one garden. The journeyman was then told to move on to a promotion which his own Old Man had secured for him in another good garden. Ultimately he rose to Foreman, and finally Head Gardener if good enough. All this was managed on the old-boy network. So to be thrown out of the scheme was serious indeed. In fact, through fear, that rarely happened. The system amounted to a formidable training board of yesteryear.

There were many lessons to be learned which are not outmoded even now, 50 years later. One came to know, for example, what a buoyant atmosphere was by the sensation as one walked into a house. It is remarkably difficult to define – a mixture of pleasant warmth and fresh air arising from a skilful manipulation of the ventilators, the heating system and the spraying of water on the floors and walls. It is the mark of a craftsman and instantly recognizable to the experienced gardener as he walks into a greenhouse. You will rarely find poor plants growing in such an atmosphere. Another important experience – laughable in retrospect – was my first encounter with the art of mixing growing composts.

Our Head Gardener was a tiny man, proud possessor of a three-speed bicycle for silent transport around the gardens and a huge turnip watch which he held in his hand as he checked in each member of his staff at 7.00 a.m. It was one of his conceits that he had a secret formula for the growing of chrysanthemums. On the great day when they were moved on to their final potting into 8 or 9 in. pots, having seen that ample supplies of Kettering loam, leaf-mould, sharp sand, powdered mortar rubble and sundry natural fertilizers were available in the potting shed, all were banished from the scene and behind the closed door the miraculous brew was mixed to the formula. This he kept in the back of his turnip watch which in turn rested in a waistcoat pocket well sprinkled with celery seed to ward off rheumatism. The mixture grew marvellous chrysanthemums and for years I believed it necessary to have distinct mixtures for most greenhouse plants. The arrival of Laurence and Newell with John Innes Composts brought a welcome commonsense to this field.

So for three decades gardeners had a standard easy formula which could be relied on to grow good plants if correctly made. But it by no means solved all the problems for the amateur. It could not cope with the man who regarded his garden soil as 'loam', or who used the cement-like fine red builders' sand or a cloddy peat well suited to a horsebox. At least these experiences ensured that one paid attention to the fact that each substance was important and had to be of the right kind.

Soon lack of loam was a problem in many lands and led to the arrival of U.C. (University of California) composts. These and many like them which followed closely were based on a peat and sand mixture with fertilizers. Such constituents were in good supply and reasonably cheap. These mixtures were a boon to the amateur, once he recognized that a new management system had to be mastered. The very light composts needed more frequent feeding and as they dried out quickly, watering became a more difficult art than ever.

Watering is probably the least understood of the gardening arts. In my early days watering by hosepipe was undreamed-of, much less tolerated. On taking over my first charge with pot plants I was provided with a tapper – a cane with a wooden hammer head about the size of a cotton reel which was long enough to reach pots at the back of the benches. Every pot from 5 in. upwards had to be tapped. A hollow sound indicated water was needed. Watering took place twice a day, so each pot was sounded twice daily. The system was necessary, as composts were much less well drained and so more sensitive to over-watering. An inviolable rule in potting was that a space be left between the soil and the top of the pot, usually $\frac{1}{2}$-1 in., so that when completely filled with water the whole of the soil ball would be moistened. Thus the twin enemies of root growth, drought and waterlogging, were avoided and a high-quality plant resulted.

To a large extent the arrival of John Innes Composts with their more gritty construction and of the plastic pot, which is unringable, saw the end of the merry ring of the watering tapper, but the fundamental principle of applying water only when needed and then adequately has never been superseded. Today one sees self-watering benches, trickle and spaghetti irrigation and other devices which are without doubt convenient and save labour but often at the expense of the quality of yesteryear.

The time came when I had to move on both to further my experience and to make room for a new journeyman at the bottom rung. It was, in fact, to a much-prized job as journeyman at the Royal Horticultural Society's Garden at Wisley in Surrey. There, five of us and the foreman lived in a bothy and were required to look after ourselves so far as feeding was concerned. We took it in turns, foreman excepted, to buy and cook our meals. At the end of the week the money spent was added up and divided by six; this was known as the 'grub score' and paid immediately we received our wages – 27 shillings a week. Woe betide the chap who spent more than the odd seven shillings on food!

There were three forms of duty extra to normal work which we were required to undertake. These were Gate Duty, simply four hours on Sunday afternoons seeing that all who entered were Fellows; Light Duty, working Saturday afternoon and Sunday up to 5.00 helping the Heavy Duty man; and Heavy Duty, the dreaded week when we were not allowed to leave the premises and were in complete charge. It was made all the more burdensome by having to ring the time bell. To start at 7.00 a.m.; breakfast 8.00 to 8.30; 12.30 to 1.30 lunch; and finally tea at 5.00. A huge bell hung on the stoke-hold chimney and pulling its chain at least released a few frustrations. The pay for each of these duties was five shillings!

Everyone today has heard of Longleat near Bath and its lions, but in Edwardian times it had one of the country's great gardens and a friend of later years told me this story of his first Christmas in 1907. That year, Christmas Day fell on a Sunday. He had entered the gardens in October and lived in a bothy with three others – the inside foreman and the first and second journeyman. He was the third journeyman. As was usual in those days, the first and second journeyman had carefully worked out the duty rota so that the new man was on duty for Christmas. At that time they worked until 4.00 p.m. on Saturday. After tea on Christmas Eve the bothy emptied rapidly and he was left on his own until Tuesday morning at 7.30 a.m. The first job was to wash up after tea. The first tour of duty round the stoke-holds was at 6.30 p.m. The duty lamp – a hurricane lamp – was supposed to be left clean and filled with oil by the previous week's duty man. This day it was empty and had a smoky glass. Having cleaned the lamp and made up the bothy fires, he sat down to read that favourite journal of the time, *The Gardeners Chronicle*, to see who had been appointed as head gardeners and to whom, and what jobs were being advertised.

Starting at 6.30 p.m., he looked in at the big vinery and the adjacent palm house. The vinery pumps were just warm to the hand and full air on; the palm house was 58°F and should have been 60°F. Into the stoke-hold he went to

make up the fire, leaving a little more draught on to pull up the missing two degrees. The propagating house, store, carnation house, orchard house and fernery all had the right temperature, so there was nothing to do in their stoke-hold other than make up the fire.

The next visit was to the early vinery and four peach houses. The vinery and one peach house were just being started into growth at 45°F; full air was on the other three. Nothing needed doing except to make up the fire. Finally there were two other fires to make up which heated the mushroom house and packing shed. So he went back to the bothy until 10.00 p.m., when the duty tour was repeated, and so to bed.

At 8.00 a.m. on Christmas morning the duty labourer came into the bothy. He had a cup of tea, after which the duty tour of houses and stoke-holds began, whilst the labourer uncovered a heated frame to pick a bunch of violets. These he took to the house a mile away for Lady Bath's breakfast tray and brought back the working requirements of the day. There were to be fourteen to dinner in the evening. Together they toured the houses, watering where necessary. After lunch they cut and prepared seven gentleman's buttonholes and seven lady's shoulder sprays. Bunches of black and white grapes, dishes of dessert apples and pears, cobnuts and walnuts were assembled, and off the labourer went to deliver them to the house and then to his home in the village.

The duty tours at 6.30 and 10.00 passed off without incident, but between, a great sin was perpetrated. He left the glasshouses! Having been invited out to an evening meal in the village, he hid the duty lamp and set off. It was necessary to hide the lamp because if the Head Gardener came to the bothy, found it in darkness and the duty lamp in its proper place he would suspect (quite rightly) that the post had been deserted. This was a terrible crime in those days, almost as bad as being found asleep on guard, the difference being the punishment: the sack rather than a court martial.

When he got back just before 10.00 p.m. he retrieved the duty lamp from an old shed, lit it and began his round. The Head Gardener had been round, for one of the doors which had been left double-locked was now single-locked, but nothing more was heard that night. However, the Head Gardener had his revenge. On Boxing night at 3.00 a.m. my friend's bedroom window was rattled by a long cane. Out of the darkness came the call 'Come on out lad! I think the wind's getting up – take a notch of air off the carnations, will you?' Amid unprintable thoughts he knew he had been rumbled.

These ramblings from the past are not quite so pointless as they might appear if we are considering the love of plants and how best to grow them. Anyone brought up in the environments we have been talking about had to interest himself in every plant that grew in the greenhouses, not just those under his care, for when duty came round he was in charge of them all. Cumulatively this became a wide knowledge of indoor plants and out of that understanding there came also a consuming love of plants which lasts a lifetime.

The garden at Wisley contains what I believe to be the widest collection of plants suited to the ordinary garden of any in Britain, and it was with reluctance that I tore myself away, or to be more accurate was ejected at the end of my studentship into a world which had three million unemployed. With great difficulty I obtained a lowly job in the nurseries of the Parks Department at Brighton, little thinking I was to spend the next 40 years, very happily, in those intensely alkaline soils.

In due time there came a chance to build a new glasshouse complete. Note that greenhouses have now become 'glasshouses' purely because, in my private vocabulary, greenhouses are made of wood and glasshouses of metal. Faced with the task of consolidating four nurseries and nine stoke-holds into one unit, I confronted the knowledge that I knew very little about what made a good glasshouse, in spite of having laboured in them for many years. In the early 1950s most new greenhouses were being build in wood, teak if you could afford it; more likely one of the then untried West African woods or western red cedar, or sometimes pine. Rarely was metal used, it being thought a cold, unhappy medium in which to grow plants. The temptation to fit the tried and trusted was great; so was the fear that I might saddle my employers with a system soon to be hopelessly outdated and a monument to my own lack of initiative. So we endeavoured to peer into the next 50 years, which is the minimum span of most greenhouse complexes. For two years I toured the country pestering the most far-seeing nurserymen and research stations. I wanted to know:

1.   Did wooden greenhouses really provide better growing conditions than metal ones and if so, why? Soon it was apparent that any difficulties there might be arose from the more rapid rise and fall of temperatures within, in response to outside conditions. This in turn was not helped by the slow response of 4 in. hot-water pipes relying on convection for circulation. I was convinced that if one had a really good heating system one could reap the benefit of the better light and lower maintenance of metal houses, without fear.

2.   Which heating system was the most efficient and cheap to run? The conventional sectional hot-water boiler feeding 10 cm (4 in.) hot-water pipes was virtually fool-proof and much to be prized because of it, but a number of rivals knocked at the door: steam in 3 cm ($1\frac{1}{4}$ in.) steel pipes; individual heaters in houses producing hot air and high-speed hot water in 5 cm (2 in.) pipes. Eventually the latter won the day. It depended on a large circulating pump which pushed the water round the circuit of an acre of glass in ten minutes with a heat loss of about 10°F on the normal water temperature of 140°F. Each house had its temperature controlled by the pipe surface provided, rather than by valves.

3.   Was it best to provide ventilation by the usual opening lights or by fans? It soon became clear that no one really understood the problems of ventilation. After two years' hard work the only worthwhile conclusion was

the impossibility of having too much, and that on conventional houses this was best supplied by continuous side and wide-opening ridge vents. Of course a multitude of unsuspected facts arose, such as that 100-120 air changes per hour would take place on a warm sunny day in a well-ventilated house, and even in mid-winter when the house was completely closed one to two changes per hour would occur through glazing imperfections.

4.   In watering plants, was there benefit in using water at house tempera-ture? This was a doctrine I had always preached and it was greatly to my chagrin that I found all the evidence was to the contrary! So we invented a never-emptying watering can by connecting flexible 1 cm (3/8 in.) rubber hosepipe to mains connections and at the business end a spray lance with instantaneous cut-off grip control. It proved easier to control than the normal watering can and enabled a reduction in the staff by two. It also enabled that fertile source of disease, the water tank, to be dispensed with.

You may have concluded that in the course of this exercise we threw out all the empiric skills of our forefathers in the light of scientific advance. But it was not so. All we had really done was to make life easier. Watering was still an art, one still needed a buoyant atmosphere, plants still responded to knowledgeable care. It is not difficult to buy a fully automated greenhouse today; given an electricity supply it can heat, water and ventilate itself. However, relatively few amateurs can afford either the initial capital or the running costs. More importantly perhaps, it undermines the belief that the love of growing plants is founded in the caring for them. These skills are tested to their limit when the problems of a cold greenhouse are tackled. Problems indeed: no heat save what may be trapped by closing the vents in early afternoon and hoping that not too much has seeped away by next morning. It is fatal in such a house to have too much water in the atmosphere in the spring, so watering and damping become critical judgements. So are dates of sowing. Wise is he who only aims at a modest improvement on what is possible in the open and who chooses plants happy at low temperatures – auriculas, carnations etc. – or to produce cut flowers or foliage undamaged by wind or rain.

Down such paths lies contentment.

Testing for Tenderness

Peter Wood, N.D.H.

Eccremocarpus scaber

O NE OF THE great challenges for the true plantsman is to succeed in growing some of those plants generally recognized as being on the borderline of hardiness. I remember well being thrilled to see good plants of *Agave americana* 'Marginata' growing out of doors the year round in the Ventnor Botanic Garden on the Isle of Wight and having recently acquired a small cottage garden in the same area, I was fired with ambition to grow some of these tender exotics.

Just as I was getting things under way, along came the terrible winter of 1978-79, which rather shattered my dreams. However, out of my experiences, I have learnt a lot which I will try to summarize here along with observations that have been given to me from up and down the country.

Until last winter, we had been fortunate in having fifteen or sixteen relatively mild winters and we may possibly have kidded ourselves that a great many plants were more hardy than was at once thought – after all camellias and fuchsias were regarded as greenhouse subjects not so long ago!

The scene after the long winter was so depressing that many people felt that it really was a waste of time trying out such plants for hardiness. But now that many plants are recovering I think we will look back on the winter as a minor setback. After all, have we not had the fun of growing these plants for a decade and a half, and can we not expect another similar period with mild winters? If we can keep a cistus or hebe for fifteen years, I think we have had good value from them – such losses are certainly well worth replacing without any delay.

My idea of having a fine large specimen of *Agave americana* on my south wall near Yarmouth on the Isle of Wight is not likely to materialize. The plant was frozen solid in the winter and it turned to mush. I have, however, a young plant to try again.

At Ventnor, many opuntias and agaves have come through, many benefiting from light shade above. This goes to show how important shelter and situation are on the ability of a plant to stand the cold.

My garden is situated in a dip but protected with a huge bank and trees from the ferocity of sea winds. Being so close to the sea, there is very little frost and so this is an ideal place to try out a variety of fascinating exotics from New Zealand and many other countries. The biggest problem is salt-laden winds, not low temperatures.

Where my own plants were protected from wind they came through practically unharmed; particularly a young *Pittosporum tenuifolium* which is now in full growth again. *Eucalyptus gunnii* had not yet grown above the screen and this too is fine, but close by a young *Acacia pravissima* was killed outright. In Dorset, not far away, a taller bush of pittosporum in a more exposed place was killed to the ground. At Ventnor, *P. tobira* lost a lot of leaves. *Cheiranthus* (*Erysimum*) 'Bowles' Purple' (also known as 'Bowles' Mauve') is not usually very long-lived but I thought I would have it for a few years in a sunny spot and well-drained soil. This was killed stone dead, and so was *Dimorphotheca ecklonis* close by.

In a neighbouring garden on a south wall, *Clematis armandii* came through well and was flowering in April. *Rosa banksiae* covering the whole of a wall also came through well. Against a more exposed wall, a clianthus was dead and myrtle was badly cut back.

It is well known that eucalypts make poor root systems and I think that they are more successful when stooled. It also seems that treated in this way they stand the winter better. At Ventnor, *Eucalyptus perriniana* appeared hardly damaged but was flowering normally in July, and yet tall specimens of *E. globulus* looked blasted in early spring but are now well on the way to recovery.

The snow gum, *E. niphophila*, came through well here and also at the Hillier Arboretum near Winchester. One of the best specimens of *Cornus capitata* I knew grew beside the open air theatre at Dartington Hall in Devon. I don't know how this fared, but there is also a good specimen at Ventnor. This came through well despite being blasted and should have flowered well.

I was surprised that *Abutilon megapotamicum* 'Variegatum' on a south wall in Woking came through so well. A lot of wood was killed but it was in full leaf again by high summer. At Ventnor, *A.* × *suntense* 'Jermyns', a large shrub, was fine and so was one of its parents, *A. ochsenii*. Not surprisingly, I have a report from Scotland that *A. megapotamicum* did not survive, but *A. vitifolium* appeared to be sprouting from the base.

Scottish gardeners also confirm reports from most parts of the country that evergreen ceanothus have fared very badly although the deciduous 'Gloire de Versailles' was hardly damaged. However, most have survived at Ventnor although they suffered greatly from salt winds.

The hebes have on the whole suffered badly. The toughest are the small-leaved kinds and the whipcords such as *H. cupressoides* have survived well. The larger-leaved types such as the beautiful red 'Simon Deleaux' have all gone. In Dorset, a huge bush of 'Midsummer Beauty' was covered in flowers in the summer of 1978 but had to be consigned to the bonfire twelve months later – it refused to produce even a single new shoot from the base!

Acacia dealbata has survived for many years in many southern gardens, and at Bembridge and Ryde on the Isle of Wight they are a sight to see early in the year. They lost a good specimen in 1977 at Ventnor because of salt winds but *A. pravissima* survived and also *A. mucronata*. Jersey did not have such low temperatures in the winter and *A. dealbata* is fine there. Arthur Hellyer tells me that he had a big bush of *Datura sanguineum* in the open – how I envy him – but this was cut back to the ground. However, he now finds it is sprouting strongly from the base.

Embothrium, the Chilean fire bush, is normally confined to very mild gardens, but the 'Norquinco' form has proved itself to be a really tough customer. I saw it flowering well at Harlow Car, Harrogate, in June and this could not be called a mild garden.

Pittosporum tenuifolium

Time and time again there are instances where a plant in an exposed position is killed and yet a similar more sheltered plant, just round the corner, survives. In Sussex, a plant of *Eccremocarpus scaber* on an east wall succumbed, but another survived happily on a south wall in the same garden.

There were fears that the famous 'palm' trees (*Cordyline*) in Devon and Cornwall had been killed. What happened was that water froze solid in the centre of the leaf rosettes. This happened with one of my plants too, but the news now is good. They are all recovering.

Phormiums have very much come into fashion in recent years, particularly since the introduction from New Zealand of new cultivars. In most parts of the country they suffered badly, but Roy Lancaster at Winchester tells me that his plants, although decimated, are sprouting again from the roots. He also has good news of a 35 ft high *Drimys*. The leaves all turned grey but the whole tree had sprung into new life by July. He was also excited to find *Beschorneria yuccoides* coming to life again after six months of apparent deadness! This same plant not only survived at Ventnor but was pushing out a flower spike in April.

Some of Ventnor's other successful exotics include *Citrus* 'Myer's Lemon', bananas, protea and crotons but although they fruit, these never develop far, not because of the weather, but because of inquisitive visitors!

Edgworthia papyrifera is not a well-known plant but it grows happily close to a high wall at Ventnor with some fine old camellias. The fragrant flower 'balls' of yellow and white appear in March and April before the leaves have developed. The winter seemed to have very little effect on it and it was flowering normally in the following spring. Incidentally, it is used in Japan for making special paper for currency.

One of the most interesting reports I received was from a reader of *Amateur Gardening* living in Bath. She was, justifiably, very proud of her 12 ft specimen of the New Zealand kowhai, *Sophora tetraptera*, a fine tree with golden yellow flowers. At the end of April it appeared dead, but by June it had burst into full flower and was a glorious sight.

I would have expected the bottle-brushes to have been killed but my own plant on a south wall, although a little battered after the winter, has grown away well since. *Choisya*, the Mexican orange, is a fine garden plant and I would have expected to hear that it too had suffered. Reports up and down the country suggest that it is a lot tougher than I expected.

Following such a hard winter I would have expected there to be many losses among the bulbous plants that I have always regarded as being 'tender'. I have, in fact, not heard of any! My own plants of *Crinum powellii* have continued to flourish and started to flower in early August.

The Headbourne *Agapanthus* hybrids are supposed to be tough and they certainly lived up to their reputation, flowering well this year with the crinums. *Nerine bowdenii*, too, has not been affected.

It is clear to me that really good soil drainage is the most important factor in keeping these bulbous plants through the winter. Where losses occur is in wet, sticky soil, and the plants die from the wet rather than low temperatures.

I discovered an excellent example of this at Harlow Car where John Main showed me a beautiful clump of semi-double *ranunculus asiaticus* in full flower in early July. They were growing in a raised bed with excellent drainage and had not minded the low temperatures one bit.

I have always regarded tigridias as plants for the milder areas of the country – they seem to flourish particularly well in the Channel Islands. However, I have had a good clump of them for several years in Surrey and by giving one or two liquid feeds in the summer they have increased very well. Whether it is my imagination or not, they even seem to be flowering better after the hard winter!

Yes, the winter of 1978-79 was a setback to plant lovers but six months after the devastation it is quite clear that where plants appeared dead, they are sprouting again and should soon recover. There have been losses, certainly, but not so many as we thought at one stage. Those that have been lost can – and should – be replaced. And let us hope that we will have another long spell of mild winters so that we can have more fun growing many more tender exotics.

The Delights
of Herbaceous
Perennials

Arthur Hellyer, M.B.E., F.L.S., V.M.H., A.H.R.H.S.

Helleborus orientalis

ANYONE who really wants to have fun with plants should choose herbaceous perennials. Shrubs may be fine for permanence, but the very fact that they are there for keeps means that, once they have been chosen and planted, there is little personal involvement in growing them.

With herbaceous plants it is quite different. Each has its own life span and its own rhythm of growth. Some, like the hellebores and the peonies, make slow progress and are best left alone for years. Others, the Michaelmas daisies among them, grow so fast that they can be lifted and divided annually, and many gardeners think this is the best way to grow them. There are short-lived perennials like the lupins and delphiniums which wear themselves out by the prodigality of their display in a few years or so and must be frequently renewed from seed or cuttings. By contrast, there are others, like the rambling acanthus and some species of polygonum, which seem to be eternal since they are constantly renewing themselves by spreading outwards and only need to be prevented from making a take-over bid for the whole garden.

So one must get to know one's herbaceous plants and learn to work with them. There is always something to do and quite often something fresh to be discovered. As a group herbaceous plants have a range that is formidable so that it is possible to spend a lifetime devoted to their cultivation and still not have mastered all that there is to know about them. Small wonder that a society is devoted especially to them as a class, and that there are also several specialist societies, including the Delphinium Society and the Iris Society, which find sufficient to sustain the enthusiasm of their members in one genus alone.

If you garden with herbaceous perennials it is relatively easy to change your plans and alter the arrangement of your garden or the balance and character of your collection. Years ago there was a famous amateur gardener, Canon Ellacombe of Bitton Rectory, Gloucestershire, who used to replant his garden every seven years or so because there were so many plants he wanted to grow and his garden was far too small to grow them all at the same time. It would be far more difficult to carry out a complete change of scenery like that with shrubs than with herbaceous perennials.

It is a pity that the term 'herbaceous border' was ever invented. I do not know who was responsible, maybe William Robinson who had a special affection for these plants, particularly if they came from the temperate zone of the northern hemisphere. He liked his plants to be hardy and he had a deep suspicion, by no means ill-founded, that most of those that came from south of the equator were likely to be unreliable in the unstable climate of the British Isles. He also liked to pontificate about the way in which plants should be used and the herbaceous border was one of his favourite devices.

The catch is that even in his day they very seldom were true herbaceous borders if by that is meant borders devoted exclusively to hardy herbaceous perennials. They were flower borders in which herbaceous plants pre-dominated but usually with shrubs, sub-shrubs, roses, annuals, biennials, climbers and bedding-out plants to help them on their way if they could contribute something desirable to the ensemble. In the 1950s we all started talking about 'mixed borders' as though we had invented something new, but flower borders had nearly all been mixed from the time they were first used, and that was long before William Robinson came on the scene.

Some people think that a true herbaceous plant must die down each autumn and reappear in the spring. A great many do just that but there are plenty of others that are evergreen or partially so and sometimes this difference will appear within a single genus, cutting it in two from a purely horticultural point of view. That is true of agapanthus, the handsome African lilies some species of which retain their leaves all winter while others lose them. It is not, perhaps, surprising that the deciduous species and hybrids are the hardiest since those that are evergreen offer their leaves as hostages to the fickle British winter.

There are a few hardy herbaceous plants that manage to reverse the seasons. One is that excellent foliage plant *Arum italicum*, which looks like a particularly fine cuckoo-pint (*Arum maculatum*) except that its shining green arrow-shaped leaves have white veins to enliven their colour. The odd, and highly useful thing about *A. italicum* is that it produces a fresh crop of leaves each autumn, retains them all winter when they are most welcome and then allows them to die away in spring when there are plenty of other things growing up to take their place.

Gertrude Jekyll, who, at the turn of the century, wrote more good sense about the association of plants than anyone before or since, used to recommend planting herbaceous perennials in rather narrow drifts, so assorted that as one passed out of flower another would take over and screen its barrenness. Modern gardens are seldom sufficiently large to permit this to be done but we have learned to think far more about foliage and be less dependent on flowers, and herbaceous plants are unrivalled in offering a wide choice of good leaves. Just think for a moment what hostas, bergenias, rodgersias, artemisias, stachys, thalictrums, dicentras, alchemillas and lots of ornamental grasses do for our gardens and how very much poorer they would be without them. Foliage is there for months on end, whereas flowers usually only continue for a few weeks. The colour of flowers can be very welcome when it comes but it is unwise to rely on it too much unless there are parts of the garden that can be planted for purely seasonal effect.

Another device for extending the floral display in borders is to plant some late-flowering plants, with tall flexible stems, towards the back and then in August or September, draw them forward with stakes or strings so that they lean over the shorter, earlier-flowering plants in front and screen their lack of beauty. The tall cultivars of *Aster cordifolius* with large sprays of small flowers and whippy stems are excellent for this purpose, but few nurserymen nowadays seem to stock these very graceful plants.

There are some herbaceous perennials that one values mainly for their good

Eryngium alpinum

communal qualities, the fine display they can make when standing shoulder to shoulder, and others so highly individualistic that it would be a shame to hide their quality in the anonymity of a crowd. In the former category I would place a great many of the daisy family including the heleniums, most but not quite all the rudbeckias (*Rudbeckia maxima* with very large black cones in the centre of each circle of golden petals is a splendid individualist), many sunflowers (but not *Helianthus* 'Monarch', a very striking plant but difficult to retain in winter), all coreopsis with the solitary exception of graceful little *Coreopsis verticillata* (which bears masses of small yellow flowers over ferny foliage), erigerons and all the perennial asters. Phloxes also belong to this class of what one might call 'broad bush' plants useful to make the bold effects, and so do all forms of *Salvia superba*, *Stachys grandiflora*, *Monarda didyma*, nepeta and most of the hardy geraniums. Many of these are indispensable plants which contribute a great deal to the well-planned garden, yet they are not the ones to go and gloat over when a particularly knowledgeable friend has to be conducted around the garden.

For these occasions, and for one's own particular delight, specialities are required such as the lovely dieramas and the strangely beautiful eryngiums. *Dierama pulcherrima* is the species usually grown, a marvellously graceful plant with long, wand-like stems (it is often called the wand flower) arching beneath the weight of little trails of purple bells. The colour is variable and at the Slieve Donald Nurseries in Northern Ireland, now sadly defunct, some specially fine seedlings were selected and given bird names. 'Heron' was one of the best, a deep reddish purple, and 'Plover' was another good one. I hope that someone is looking after them because it would be sad if they were lost. There are other species besides *D. pulcherrima*, one of them, named *D. cooperi*, much shorter and more erect but with the same type of flower. It could be a parent for a race of dwarf wand flowers for the middle and front positions in the flower border.

The eryngiums are, of course, the sea hollies, one of them widely distributed around our own coast where its long tap roots enable it to thrive even in deep sand dunes. The loveliest is *Eryngium alpinum*, a much taller plant, up to 3 ft (90 cm) high, with the typical teazle-like flower heads surrounded by steely blue bracts divided like fine lace. I put it in the 'super plant' class.

All the veratrums are of high quality. Their leaves are a delight: large, broadly spear-shaped and pleated like a fan. Slugs are fond of them and will riddle them with holes if one does not take due care. The flowers are quite exceptional, small but numerous, crowded in stiffly erect branched spikes. They are an intensely deep maroon, almost black, in *Veratrum nigrum*, lime green in *V. viride*, which seems to be the easiest species to acquire, and eau-de-nil in *V. album*. No one is likely to pass by these plants in the garden without comment or enquiry.

The same is true of the foxtail lilies (*Eremurus*), but with these it is the flowers that are the sole attraction, the strap-shaped leaves being fairly ordinary and dying down quite early in the summer. The flowers are arranged in dense spikes crowning sturdy bare stems which grow straight up from the clump in a manner not dissimilar to that of the red hot pokers or kniphofias. *Eremurus robustus* is the giant of the family, with flower stems a good 2.5 m high, half of this bearing the satin pink flowers. *E. bungei* is one of the smallest, a mere yard (metre) high, with yellow flowers. Botanists appear to be doubtful about the name and say it is probably a garden form of *E. stenophyllus*, which certainly looks much like it. There is similar uncertainty about *E. elwesii*, close to 6½ ft (2 metres) high, varying in colour from white to pink. Some say that it is a smaller variant of *E. robustus*, others that it is a taller form of *E. himalaicus*, which has white flowers. Gardeners who are interested in botany can have fun trying to sort out these confusions for themselves, but for most the names matter little, it is the beauty that counts. And perhaps the best way to enjoy that is to forget the species altogether and concentrate on the acknowledged hybrids, such as the Shelford Hybrids, all of medium height and varying in colour from pale yellow through apricot to light orange and pink.

All these foxtail lilies make extraordinary roots, fleshy and radiating widely like the spokes of a wheel from a central crown, or cluster of crowns, which bear all the buds from which the growth comes. These roots hate being disturbed, so these are plants for which as permanent a position as possible should be sought. They like well-drained soil overlying chalk or limestone, but I do not think that the lime is essential for I have seen them thriving in sandy soils that were almost certainly moderately acid. The best way to propagate them is by seed but this can take time to germinate and several years to flowering. Old plants with several crowns can be lifted and very carefully divided but it is not easy without losing some of the fleshy roots.

Much of the breeding of the foxtail lilies has been done by amateurs, and the same is true of several other genera of hardy herbaceous perennials. In fact if you fancy yourself as a plant breeder it is probable that these plants will provide the most promising material. Almost all the wonderfully varied June-flowering irises have been raised in private gardens, and the same is true of the day lilies (*Hemerocallis*) which have become a cult in the U.S.A. Both iris and hemerocallis have large flowers with clearly identifiable sexual organs, so that it is easy to see what one is about. Seed germinates readily, though it may take a few years for the seedlings to mature and reveal their quality. But once a breeding programme is under way there will be a new batch to assess each season to maintain interest and determine whether one is proceeding in the right direction.

Amateurs have also played a big role in the development of delphiniums and some of them actually turned professional as a result of their success. Now that the big nursery firms that once specialized in delphiniums have either closed down or are turning increasingly to other lines, the role of the amateur seems likely to become increasingly important.

But if I wanted to start a breeding programme with perennials I would look for something that has been less well developed. Some people are already busily working with hostas and hellebores and I wonder when someone will decide to have a go at euphorbias and camassias, both with plenty of species crying out for development.

A few breeders have shown what wonderful things can be done with alstroemerias but, with the exception of the Ligtu Hybrids, the results of their labours remain firmly in the hands of commercial cut-flower producers who jealously guard their treasures and will not permit them to reach the retail plant market. So here is another rich vein, proved in worth but waiting to be fully exploited. The most promising species would appear to be *Alstroemeria haemantha* (but it might be difficult to find the true species with yellow, orange and purple flowers), *A. ligtu* in various shades of pink, and *A. violacea* with violet-purple and yellow flowers. *A. pulchella*, often called *A. psittacina*, with red flowers tipped with green, could also be useful but it comes from Brazil (the others are all natives of Chile) and so could scarcely be called hardy. Still, it might bequeath to hybrids its distinctive colouring without its tenderness and that, after all, is what breeding is all about.

It is time, too, that someone took another look at peonies. There are a lot of lovely species that have never been used in any breeding programme and, except in America, precious few breeders who have been doing anything about this marvellous genus, so good in flower and foliage, over the last 30 years or so. What about the delightful yellow shades that might be coaxed out of *Paeonia mlokosewitschii*, itself one of the most beautiful of all herbaceous plants, so lovely, indeed, that it seems almost sacrilegious to suggest using it in a breeding programme. How could it possibly be improved? The answer, of course, is that it could not, but breeding is not solely about 'improvement', whatever that may mean. It is much more about variation, about creating something that never existed before and which could have a value for some particular purpose. *P. tenuifolium* is another that might be used in the hope that it would pass on its elegant finely divided foliage to some of its offspring combined with more robust, longer-lasting flowers.

And then there are the plants that were once favourites but have somehow dropped out of the running so that it is actually hard to find them nowadays. What happened, for example, to all the sweet violets once in such demand that several small nurseries devoted the whole of their attention to them? Maybe too much emphasis was placed on size of flower and length of stem and not enough on hardiness and constitution. It would be worth looking at 'Admiral Avallon', 'Czar' and 'Coeur d'Alsace' again, the last with lovely soft pink flowers, and a fine performer outdoors. Starting with these and similar hardy cultivars as a base, there would never be any doubt of the ability of their offspring to survive and flower outdoors.

The double primroses, which at one time looked like sharing the fate of the violets, are actually well on their way back thanks to the cleverness of someone who has discovered how to produce them from seed so that good strains can be constantly renewed without being debilitated by age and the insidious build-up of viruses so likely to occur in vegetatively propagated plants.

A great many herbaceous perennials can be increased most conveniently by division, the simplest method of propagation requiring no special apparatus and no great degree of skill. It is pleasant to be able to multiply stock readily so that plants are always available to be given to admiring visitors or maybe to help out at some local fête or bazaar. Nor is there any close season for division, for though March and April may be the most favourable months, with September and October running them close except for awkward customers like the Caucasian scabious and the Amellus forms of Michaelmas daisy, it is possible to divide most herbaceous perennials at any time of the year if one is prepared to take a few extra precautions and accept a few losses. A very skilful gardener I knew used to make what she called a dunce's cap for any plant given to her out of season: a cone of newspaper which she placed over the plant for the first few weeks to shield it from the sun and wind while it was taking root. Nowadays I would prefer to use plastic bags or cloches, either of which retain moisture better than paper without cutting ŏff so much light.

But even with devices like this, division is not the answer to all propagation of herbaceous perennials. It will not do at all for the tap-rooted kinds such as gypsophilas, verbascums, anchusas, lupins and hollyhocks, and it is not very satisfactory for plants that make tough crowns as do delphiniums and *Scabiosa caucasica*. Cuttings are often the right answer for these if they cannot be increased satisfactorily from seed. The latter is always a good way to increase plants since seedlings start with a new lease of life, and usually complete freedom from parental pests and diseases, which is much more difficult to achieve with any form of vegetative propagation. But good stem cuttings of herbaceous plants may only be available for a very short time, usually in spring when the young growth is extending rapidly. Basal shoots should be severed close to roots or crown with the certainty that the base of the cutting will be solid flesh right through, not hollow as it probably will be a few weeks later.

Some herbaceous plants grow well from root cuttings and it is not only the obvious kinds, with thick, plunging roots like the verbascums, anchusas and oriental poppies, that are suitable candidates for this method. Phloxes and gaillardias grow freely from root cuttings even though their roots are relatively thin; it is a particularly good way to increase phloxes, which are subject to attacks by eelworms, as these live in the stems and the roots are usually quite free of them. If you take a large kitchen knife and scoop out the whole centre of a phlox plant in September or October and then fill the shallow, cup-shaped hole you have made with peat and sand, scores of shoots will come sprouting up in the spring direct from the severed roots. The plant can then be lifted and will literally fall apart into rooted pieces each of which will grow on rapidly into a fine plant.

Thoughts on Herbs

Ann Bonar

Bay   Parsley   Garlic   Thyme

F OR ME, the seed of herbal interest must have been sown when I first heard the story, as a child, of the mandrake, *Mandragora officinarum*. You will remember that it was said to let out such a terrible shriek when it was dug up that anyone who heard it died instantly. To avoid this, a hungry dog was tied to the plant, and a plate of meat put near to it. Then, with any luck, the plant would be pulled out of the ground and the unfortunate dog would die.

Of all the herbs, the mandrake is one of those most invested with magic and legends; its curiously forked, tuberous roots can have an uncanny resemblance to the human body and, amongst other beliefs, it was thought to cure sterility, to guard against bad luck and to act as an anaesthetic. In fact, the fresh root is an emetic and purgative, and the leaves can be used as a poultice for ulcers.

I must admit that one of the chief charms of herbs for me is the mysterious atmosphere that surrounds them. They are the oldest of the cultivated plants, and this must be part of the reason for the tremendous accumulation of myths concerning their use down the centuries. Many of the stories, on the face of it, are ludicrous, but many also have a grain of truth in them. Originally herbs were deliberately grown for their medicinal properties and, since faith in one's doctor has a good deal to do with curing ill-health, the apothecaries of old concealed the often simple truth beneath elaborate rituals, rather on the same principle that if a medicine tastes foul, it must be good for you.

There are so many of these legends: the elderberry which kept away witches if planted outside the front door; rosemary which cured baldness and bad dreams; and garlic which was said to lure moles from the soil. Vervain, one of the favourite herbs of the Druids, was worn as a charm against headaches.

Basil seems to have caused a great deal of controversy, none of the old herbalists being able to agree as to whether it was good or bad. Culpeper remarked in his herbal that: 'This is the herb which all authors are together by the ears about and rail at one another like lawyers . . . with downright Billingsgate rhetoric'.

The idea of woad being used by our Celtic forebears as a body paint is firmly entrenched in modern minds, but it was probably used, not for ornament, but to stop wounds bleeding, as it is a good styptic. As a source of blue dye, it was still being milled in Lincolnshire as late as 1939.

No other group of plants has this extraordinary agglomeration of truths, legends and half-superstitious, half-genuine beliefs surrounding it. Such a quality will have its own appeal for many non-gardeners.

The original herbal fascination led to a curiosity about herbs in general, and I discovered many had another characteristic which I particularly like in plants: that of fragrance or aroma. Lavender, roses, violets, orris root, jasmine – these are all herbs – their perfumes intangibly delightful, and tantalizing in their invisibility.

The herbal aromatics, having more body, are more satisfying – you can feel the pungency of rosemary, sharp and cool, as it trickles up inside your forehead to your brain. Thyme, mint, marjoram and tarragon also have distinctive and powerfully pleasing odours which rightly make them good cooking additives, quite apart from any medicinal or digestive properties. Some are very peculiar, not to say unpleasant: for instance rue, the leaves once rubbed and their bitter, acrid aroma inhaled, is never forgotten. It was once thought to do great things for poor eyesight. Chamomile is aromatic, but not really pleasant, and the medicinal hyssop tastes better than it smells; it is said to 'improve the tone of a feeble stomach'.

The aromatic quality of herbs made itself most felt for me during a visit to Crete one spring. We were mostly walking in the foothills and mountains, and I came to the conclusion that the Cretan countryside is one vast natural herb-cum-rock garden. In the same way that the air in the Austrian Tyrol is always pine-scented, so in Crete one cannot take in air without absorbing a blend of herbal fragrances as well. One tramples them underfoot on the paths, or brushes against them while walking; go into a local market and your nose will tell you instantly where the herb stalls are.

The Mediterranean herbs growing in their native habitat have a much greater strength of aroma than in Britain, a sweet, spicy, smoky quality brought out by the sun's heat. The Cretan species of thyme, *Thymus capitatus*, is particularly distinctive and a whiff of this in a sachet of mixed herbs brings back instantly the heat, the sun, the peace and friendliness of the island.

Herbs grow so abundantly naturally in Crete, about the only kind of useful plant that does, that they are bound to play a large part in Cretan everyday life, where the mountainous terrain makes farming and growing sparse and difficult. A request for tea produces a brew made from the leaves of false dittany, *Ballota acetabulosa*, rather than the more familiar Indian infusion.

Spit-roasted lamb or kid will be thickly covered with thyme and/or rosemary, and a plate of the local snails will have marjoram scattered over it.

The true dittany, *Origanum dictamnus*, is still much used medicinally; if you go in June or July, you will see the pink flowers in clusters, looking exactly like small pink hops. Another good health herb is French lavender, *Lavandula stoechas*, which blankets the stony hillsides from March to June, its strong perfume providing a powerful deterrent to biting and stinging insects.

Although culinary herb cultivation and use went out of fashion after the Second World War, the last decade has produced a great, one might say a growing, revival. The enthusiasm for parsley never really died, and it has provided the link between the past and present, to which other herbs have been gradually attached – mint, thyme and sage, then rosemary and bay, followed by chives, marjoram, basil and tarragon, and now coriander, dill, fennel, caraway, sorrel, chervil and savory. Most of these are automatically listed in the current catalogues of leading seedsmen, and there are at least a dozen specialist herb nurseries providing a much greater selection, both as seeds and as plants.

Mint   Rosemary   Sage   Chamomile   Winter savory

Most herbs are easily grown. If they come from the Mediterranean area give them shelter, sun, poor well-drained soil, preferably stony, and protect them from prolonged hard frost if shrubby. Do not give them normal dressings of concentrated fertilizers, as they become too lush and lose most of their essential oils. Grow them 'hard' – you can give the soil a little rotted manure or garden compost as a mulch or dug in, or a light dressing of a slow-acting organic fertilizer such as hoof and horn, but nothing else.

Some herbs like quite different conditions of growth – parsley, mint, angelica, borage, lovage all prefer moist, deep soil and a little shade, though they will survive in ordinary soils and some sun. Many herbs which are plants native to Britain, commonly called weeds, will grow anywhere without any special treatment, for instance eyebright, dandelion and sweet cicely.

Plant outdoors in April, and sow seed in August-September or April. Many herb seeds are only viable for a little while after ripening, and as they flower in July-August, so late summer or early autumn is the best time to sow. Angelica, chervil, lovage and savory come into this category.

As with all young plants, it pays to eliminate the weeds which germinate with the herbs, so that the latter have a chance to consolidate and mature. Thinning will be necessary if you did not sow and plant out in peat pots.

Herbs in full growth need little care; supporting and tying will be necessary for some, and removal of old flowered stems will improve their appearance. Pests and diseases rarely infest herbs, one of their leading attractions for gardeners.

If you are thinking of drying the leaves and flowers, the best time to strip the leaves is just before the plant is due to flower. If the flowers are to be preserved, the petals should be taken just as the flowers are completely expanded. Gather early on a dry sunny morning to ensure the maximum content of essential oils. The drying which follows should be done in the dark, with good ventilation, and quickly, provided the plant material is not reduced to a crisp; a temperature of between 21 and 36°C (70 and 90°F) is ideal.

In spite of their great fascination one has to admit that many herbs are not outstandingly beautiful. The culinary and medicinal herbs in particular are mostly utilitarian in appearance, and this could have been one of the reasons for the development of the knot or maze garden of mediaeval times. The geometric patterns of the beds provided the visual interest, and the low-growing clipped edgings of box, curry plant or santolina (cotton lavender) gave the plants they enclosed the definition they needed, without which they could easily become a woolly amorphous mass of vegetation. This must also be why they look so attractive growing amongst the formal surroundings of paths paved with brick, stone or cobbles, or carpeted with gravel or sand.

Designing a good herb garden is not as easy as it looks at first sight, but there are all sorts of possibilities. A circular garden with the paths forming the spokes of a wheel, and a sundial in the centre, is simple and appropriate. The chessboard plan is another neat way of growing herbs, planting a different species in alternate squares, and using every other square for a marking plant, perhaps southernwood or creeping thyme. I have always liked the idea of growing herbs in groups, i.e. medicinal kinds in one bed, aromatic in another, cosmetic in a third and culinary in a fourth. One could also grow them in plant families – the labiates, the borages and the umbellifers are three which contain a lot of different herb species. For the literary, collecting the herbs mentioned in Shakespeare's plays could result in all sorts of unexpected visits and explorations in search of plants.

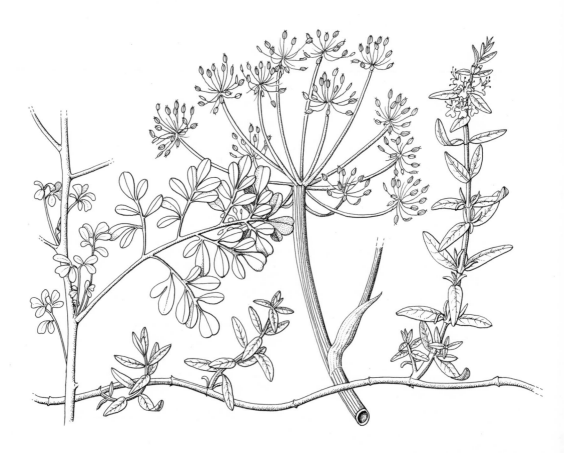

Rue   *Angelica*   *Hyssop*

There are herb gardens tucked away all over the country whose designs will provide inspiration and ideas to spark off your own imagination. The famous one at Sissinghurst Castle in Kent is particularly well laid-out and cared for; there are others at Claverton Manor, Somerset, Knole in Kent, the Royal Horticultural Society's Garden at Wisley in Surrey, Hardwick Hall in Derbyshire, and Lullingstone Castle, Eynsford, Kent.

The gardens of the monastic orders of the Middle Ages were the main sources of cultivated herbal plants. They are marked on extant plans as 'physick' gardens, though they were not, as were the fruit trees in one plan, planted in the graveyard. With the dissolution of the monasteries, the herb gardens to some extent were transferred, in design, if not in plants, to the Oxford and Cambridge colleges, and today collections of herbal plants are still maintained at the botanic gardens of each university.

Visiting the herb nurseries is much more rewarding than ordering by post, as many stock and sell plants unlisted in their catalogues because they have too few for general demand. Some run talks or one-day courses on such varied subjects as cooking, growing, pot-pourris, wine-making, herb cultivation in other countries, medicinal herbs, and the old herbals.

Of course, there are some highly ornamental herbs. Some of the old shrub roses are herbs; their main uses were in medicine and perfumery. For instance, have you ever wondered how the dog rose, *Rosa canina*, got its name? One explanation is that the roots would cure rabies or the infection resulting from the bite of a mad dog. One thing is certain – the hips of the dog rose are an excellent source of vitamin C, as witness the manufacture of rose-hip syrup during the last war.

The damask rose, *R. damascena*, and the cabbage rose, *R. centifolia*, are the two species mainly used to supply otto of roses for perfumery, Grasse in France and Kazanlik in Bulgaria being two of the main centres of extraction. Vital statistics are that 30 rose blooms are needed for one drop of otto, and about 90 kg of rose flowers will result in 28 g of the oil, which is obtained by distillation.

Marigolds, nasturtiums, pelargoniums, yellow gentian, foxgloves, catmint, field poppy (*Papaver rhoeas*) and saffron are some more plants which are distinctly attractive, originally grown for a variety of reasons.

The field poppy supplies a bright red dye; the roots of yellow gentian are said to be an appetizer and a tonic. Catmint, besides being a magnet to all the cats in the district, is an excellent diaphoretic. Marigold petals were once used to colour butter and cheese, and the leaves of the aromatic varieties of pelargoniums still add distinctive and delicious flavourings to custards, milk dishes, jellies and preserves. Nasturtium seeds pickled when young are good substitutes for capers.

If you can tear yourself away from all the practical aspects of herbs: growing them, cooking with them, experimenting with curing minor ailments, trying them as dyes and for cosmetics, and begin to browse amongst the literature, you will be led into yet more interesting highways and byways.

The best of the modern books and encyclopaedias on herbs are a joy to look at, as well as to read. Beautifully designed and printed as they are, the colour illustrations have never been more exactly reproduced, while the text is packed with information obtained both from practical experience and the vast range of ancient herbals in libraries and museums.

The old herbals were the medicinal as well as the botanical textbooks of their time. The very earliest examples were illustrated mainly to provide a means of identification, rather than to add to the appearance of the book. The earliest extant is the *Codex Vindobonensis* in the National Library, Vienna (nothing if not an interesting highway down which to be led), having illustrations drawn and painted about 512 A.D., some of them probably derived from drawings by a Greek doctor, Krateuas, who lived in the first century B.C.

Two of the plants shown in the *Codex* are the opium poppy and the bramble; in Britain in the Bodleian Library, Oxford, there is another bramble illustration in colour, in an eleventh-century MS. The bramble seems to have been popular – it was drawn by no less an artist than Leonardo da Vinci in about 1507.

The herbals began to appear more abundantly with the invention of printing. Gerard's *The Herball* (1597) and Culpeper's *The English Physitian* (1652) are probably the best known, though only the former was illustrated, with wood-cuts. Culpeper's book did not have engravings added until the 1789 edition. However, the herbals gave way to books on gardening in general and the only book in recent times to approach the old style of herbal in its botanical and medicinal content, is the one by Mrs Grieve, *A Modern Herbal*, published in 1931.

A Dictionary of Herbs, edited by Dr Malcolm Stuart, until recently the Director of the Herb Society, is the most comprehensive of the current publications, and is a tribute to the printer's art as well as the designer's sense of colour and form.

Herbs and all that is associated with them have expanded not only my gardening horizons, but also my enthusiasm for so many other potential interests and pleasures – art, travel, history, medicine – that I feel, like Karel Čapek in *The Gardener's Year*: 'The gardener wants eleven hundred years to test, learn to know and appreciate fully all that is his'. At a modest estimate the subject of herbs will need at least that amount of time for me.

Bulbs on My Mind

Gillian Beckett

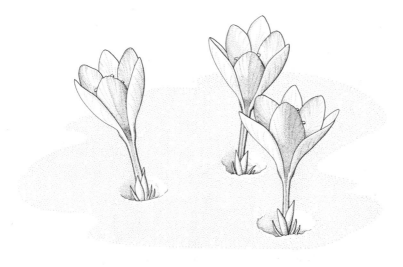

Crocus dalmaticus

E VERY INTEREST has to have a start and there are some who will point to a single happening and claim without a vestige of doubt that at that moment their world changed. For others, and I am one, things seem to begin far less dramatically and it is difficult to say when my interest in bulbs began.

Perhaps it was those unfortunate hyacinths which languished every year at school in their water glasses. They were hardly inspiring though, with their tendency to flower too soon because of the warm conditions, or to lurch drunkenly as the flower head grew too large for its minimal support. It certainly wasn't the bowls of paper white narcissus which met a similar fate each Christmas, being put in the dark under a bed where the warmth usually caused the flowers to abort. Maybe that is why I still prefer my bulbs out of doors.

In fact it was probably my first sight of crocuses flowering at the edge of early spring snow in the Alps which encouraged the initial steps down the slippery path. They were *Crocus albiflorus*, one of the earliest of the alpine crocuses, white, yet with a lustre which made them far more pure than the melting snow which almost surrounded them. The more colourful *Crocus dalmaticus* with its lilac flowers can make a similarly dramatic entrance into the world and I have memories of it with each small bloom coming through a neat, round hole melted in the snow.

This sudden release from the grip of winter, safely buried under the snow until spring sun clears it away, is something rarely attained in less well-ordered, milder climates. The first cold of winter will see the bulbs extending their roots underground, but an unseasonal mild spell can trigger off the mechanisms of growth. Up come the flowers to be greeted by a return to cold and wet. Crocuses are ill-adapted to such treatment, for the slender tube which extends up from the ground, opening into the flower proper, is not a strong stem, but a delicate fold of petals, or to be botanically correct, tepals, easily broken by the wind. Given sunshine, the flowers will open to reveal the usually colourful stamens which lead down to the all-important ovary still safely beneath the ground. As several species open in the autumn, it is quite possible to have some blooms in the garden from October to April whenever the weather is sufficiently clement.

Snowdrops too can cheer the winter days by providing a succession of flowers. Almost annually there will appear in one newspaper or another a letter asking if their snowdrop is the first one of the winter. As the letters always come in December, the answer must be no, for Queen Olga's snowdrop from Greece, *Galanthus nivalis reginae-olgae*, usually opens in October. In the Balkans are a number of early-flowering snowdrops, most of which are really little more than forms of our commonest species. Seeds collected from a clump in Jugoslavia several years ago have produced plants which flower in late November and December. They are probably G. *corcyrensis* and nicely bridge the gap to January and February when other species and many fine forms of our G. *nivalis* flower. G. *ikariae* from Greece,

Ornithogalum umbellatum   *Fritillaria meleagris*

Fritillaria tenella   *Galanthus nivalis*   *Muscari armeniacum*

with broad, bright green leaves which set off the flowers perfectly, is usually the last and my favourite.

Sowing seeds of bulbs is perhaps the most important step in the development of the enthusiast. Patience is a prime necessity, especially in the early years when a small row of compost-filled and carefully labelled pots is all that is to be seen. After some months, perhaps even a year, something green appears. Two broad seed leaves? Certainly a weed. Then comes the moment when a single green spike pokes through. For a few tantalizing days it is indistinguishable from grass – at least to the novice – but at last it becomes obvious that it is an incipient crocus, snowdrop or whatever it should be. For one whole year, that single spike will be all that appears above the ground, but the next year there may be two or more and eventually will come the day when it flowers and the wait will fade into insignificance.

After that first year it is never so bad again, for each season more seeds will go in, so there will always be a few which have survived the perils of infancy and slugs and are ready to flower. Tulips are amongst the most long-winded, some taking up to six years to reach flowering size. It is easy in this case to be tempted by the bulb catalogues which begin to fall on the mat. Just one bulb of *Tulipa urumiensis* to open its golden stars? One bulb doesn't make much of a show, better make it three. Then how about *Tulipa hageri* as a contrast with its brick-red tepals, or *T. turkestanica* which is so different with its branched stems and cream and white flowers? These so-called botanical tulips are a fascinating group and well worth growing. Most do however respond to a warm, dry summer, coming from the arid parts of the Middle East, and they don't like a carpet of ground-covering plants over them, shading the bulbs from the sun. The most satisfactory course of action is to take up any which seem to be decreasing each year and keep them dry during the summer before re-planting in the autumn. This is of course a chore, but each spring when the cheerful flowers open and do their best to obliterate memories of a harsh winter, you are well repaid.

The many species and cultivars of *Narcissus* are less fussy in this respect. Being mostly plants of woodland or moist mountain pastures, they are not adapted to any dry period and thrive best if left alone. From the giant blooms of the best trumpet daffodils to the beautiful wild forms of the hoop petticoat daffodil, *N. bulbocodium*, there is something for every taste and every garden. So many cultivars of the smaller species have been raised that it is almost impossible to keep up with them, but I will always cherish the memory of a planting of the pure white 'Thalia', growing through the bronze-purple leaves of the wood spurge *Euphorbia amygdaloides* 'Purpurea'. Of course to be really up to date there are the split-corona narcissi. These are looked upon with loathing by the purists and are indeed travesties of a true daffodil, but if looked at as quite a different species altogether, then it must be admitted that they have their attraction.

There are other bulbs which are best dried off in summer, and once the bulb bug has bitten sufficiently deep, thoughts of some of the more exacting genera of plants will intrude. Fritillaries for example. The beautiful crown imperial, *Fritillaria imperialis*, presents few problems, likewise the British native snakeshead fritillary, *F. meleagris*, but others can be less easy to grow, or at least to grow well. My introduction to other fritillaries was in Jugoslavia where *F. tenella* was growing in an area of bare limestone, one opportunist plant pushing its flower up through a small round hole in the middle of a limestone boulder, rather reminiscent of the crocuses in the snow. The chequered bells, like those of many other species, were duller outside than in, meaning that the plant looked best if viewed flat on your face, and again like its near allies, could not really be called beautiful. All have however a fascination, with their intricate marking, and demand the attention of many a would-be grower. A few species are in fact good garden plants, and *F. pyrenaica* with its deep maroon purple bells deserves to be grown more often. Like the equally uncommon scarlet *Tulipa sprengeri*, it naturalizes well in soils of all types. Most of the South European and Asiatic species are not difficult to grow and flower in pots, but the American plants are quite a different problem. As soon as the bulbs reach a reasonable size, they propagate themselves by splitting into many small ones, instead of going on to flower. So when a grower says he has 60 bulbs of *F. liliacea*, or of the bright red *F. pluriflora*, it probably just means that he hasn't yet found how to make them flower. Very long pots, those that used to be called 'long toms', are said to be one answer. My bulbs in them are growing in size, but will they flower? Every gardener is an optimist – unlike the farmer – so I await the spring with great hope.

Propagation of most bulbous plants is not difficult as most divide or produce offsets. Most, but not all. One bulb of *Muscari ambrosiacum*, a silvery-purple grape hyacinth, has flowered regularly in the garden for the last twelve years, but has failed to increase at all. It is however exceptional. The main problem for the keen beginner is getting the bulbs in the first place. Some are available from specialist nurseries, but by no means all. How then does one build up a collection? The answer is by making contact with other enthusiasts and exchanging and acquiring offsets and seed. True gardeners are amazingly generous. The various alpine and rock garden societies include small bulbs in their field of interest, as they are often grown in alpine houses or rock gardens. Their annual lists of seeds sent in by members for distribution within the society are the reason why I rush to greet the postman in the cold, dark days just after Christmas. The evening that each seedlist arrives is given over to searching for wanted plants and hopefully ringing those required. Back goes the order by the next post, then follow days of waiting until at last the packet arrives and the new treasures are opened and sown. All this helps to while away the winter and by the time the last seeds have arrived, the crocuses and fritillaries are flowering – at least some of them.

A few bulbs can become weeds in the garden and on a light sandy soil it is as well to be wary of the common grape hyacinth, *Muscari armeniacum*, which rapidly forms dense, grassy clumps and spreads around with amazing ease. In the right place it can give a blue haze like a distant bluebell wood, but amongst small plants it can be a real curse. The lovely white star of Bethlehem, *Ornithogalum umbellatum*, has similar habits, though in the right place it is beautiful. Normally it flowers at the same time as its leaves on stems several centimetres long, but after the very cold winter of 1963, its buds were so far advanced beneath the ground that they opened as soon as they pushed through the soil. If only they would do that every year, many of their sins would be forgiven them. There are of course well-behaved members of both genera and of the grape hyacinths I should be sorry not to have *M. latifolium*, the dark blue flowers held well above each strap-shaped leaf, each plant producing just one.

Summer bulbs are many, especially if you take the bulb catalogue's idea of what is a bulb, rather than that of the botanist, but they are rather overwhelmed by the general colour of the summer garden. After all, who would notice a snowdrop blooming in June – it would hardly be considered worthy of a place in the garden! Bulbs don't really come into their own again until late summer when the white bells of the stately *Galtonia candicans* demand attention. Autumn proper is heralded by the lovely pink nerines, the crocus-like yellow sternbergias and of course the colchicums, which are soon forgiven their unwieldy spring leaves when they open their shapely flowers. Sternbergias are strangely overlooked, the common *S. lutea* being showy, hardy, easy and often producing its flowers right through December. *Nerine bowdenii* is also grown less than it should be, probably because of its reputation for tenderness; it is after all South African. Given a sheltered spot at the foot of a wall or beneath high tree cover, it will come through every winter with no further protection and gives weeks of pleasure just when the rest of the garden is beginning to take on that Novemberish look.

Perhaps one of the chief delights of bulbs is their variety of colour and form, together with their small demands on space which makes them ideal for the smallest garden or greenhouse. Then of course there is the excitement of raising seeds of a species for which a description cannot be found. It will of course have an official one at places like Kew, but for us it is as good as new. Will it be colourful and rewarding or have minute off-white flowers which hardly open? It is a gamble, and as I have said before, every gardener is an optimist, so where did that seedlist from Central Asia go? What about trying *Eremurus suvorovii, Iris sogdiana, Tulipa korolkovii, Korolkovia severtzovii* . . .?

Bringing the Garden Indoors

Julia Clements, V.M.H.

A GARDEN is a lovesome thing . . .' so wrote Thomas Edward Brown and so wrote many poets, as though a garden was something to sit and be looked at. Some of us do just that, especially after the work is done, whilst many more like to bring some of the garden indoors in the shape of cut flowers, so that our gaze may be continued.

And just as colour schemes are planned for the garden and herbaceous borders are created with tall flowers at the back and shorter in front, and just as a garden designer will place a statue, sundial or seat as a focal point, so also will the flower arranger plan decorations for the house with similar principles of design in mind. With tens of thousands of men and women now practising the art of flower arranging, many still ask 'How do I start?' The answer is to study the setting. Ask yourself if you need a large arrangement for a special occasion, or a smaller one for a side table. You might need a low arrangement for the dining table, or a light-coloured design for a dark room. You might own a modern house, in which case a stark linear design would be more appropriate, or simple country flowers would be more desirable for a cottage.

So first decide what you want to do in the way of size and colour and where the flowers will stand when finished. Then, when the head of the house is not looking, go out and pick what you need. Of course if you are wise you will have a separate cutting garden. I grow lots of annuals and leafy shrubs in a portion of the kitchen garden, for here I can pick without disturbing the appearance of the main garden. It is here I grow such plants as hostas in a number of varieties, for the leaves are so useful and attractive as central interest in any design. Of course they die down in autumn, and then my *Arum italicum* leaves start to appear to take their place, these dying down in spring, just as the hostas are coming up again. In this back portion of the garden I keep bushes of *Choisya ternata* (Mexican orange blossom), for I constantly use these evergreen leaves as fillers, and for similar reasons I grow *Viburnum tinus* and *Aucuba*. I have a hedge of golden privet (*Ligustrum ovalifolium* 'Aureum') which I never clip, as it gives lovely long sprays of golden leaves which last for weeks when cut. I find this so useful for Church decorations, for its colouring will light up a dark corner anywhere. If I need sprays of leafy or flowering shrubs from the main garden, I usually cut from the back or underneath, for it is there you find twisty or swerving sprays – very necessary for the sides of large groups. And of course, the cutting often does a lot of good to the shrub itself.

So try to pick with a plan in mind; you can then avoid waste. For a large display you will sometimes, though not always, need some greenery for the background, then if you have decided upon your colour scheme, you will pick (1) some tall flowers for the outline of the shape, (2) some bigger or more important flowers for the centre, and (3) some less important flowers for filling in.

All flower stems should be recut on reaching the house and stood in deep water in a cool place for some hours or overnight before arranging them. This will allow the stems to become fully charged with water thus enabling them to last much longer. Most leaves and leafy sprays should be submerged overnight to help them become turgid and strong (I always add a tablespoonful of sugar to a shallow bath; this helps close the pores on the underside of the leaves, so avoiding too much loss of moisture through transpiration when arranged). The only exceptions to this submerging treatment are the woolly grey leaves such as *Stachys lanata* (lamb's-ears), *Onopordum acanthium* (Scotch thistle) and others which soak up water like a sponge and lose their greyness.

With your flowers strong and bright after their night's drink, fill your vase with tepid water and crumpled wire netting (2-in. mesh), or if you prefer it, use water-soaked floral foam, but whatever you choose do allow it to rise about two inches *above* the rim of the vase, in order that some of the side and front stems can be inserted almost horizontally, so allowing them to flow out and downwards. First make the height and width of your design with your tallest or thinnest flowers. You can make it what height you like, but as a guide, the tallest central stems can be one-and-a-half times higher than the height of the vase, and the sides two-thirds that of the height. Next insert the important flowers down the centre, cutting each stem shorter than the other so that no two heads stand equal to each other, and finally, fill in from the outside to the centre with the less important flowers, making sure that some of the lower flowers flow forward over the rim to avoid a flat effect. Leaves added round the centre and at the back will give depth to the finished design.

When teaching or demonstrating I am often asked what happens when only one type of flower is available. I am sure most gardens can provide some different shape or form, but if genuinely stuck with only one kind of flower, try cutting some of the stems to give you various heights such as tall, medium and short, placing them in the order of (1) outline, (2) centre, and (3) fill in. Leaves around the centre will unify the stems, and the flowers in a finished design should appear to emerge from a central point which is just over the rim underneath the tallest stem.

In bringing the garden indoors, we are often content to gaze upon, say, one beautiful head of rhododendron, or a spray of camellia. Pleasure can also be obtained from an uncontrived arrangement of a bunch of flowers all one colour. A modern design of a twisty branch and two or three tulips or roses can give delight to many in the right setting. There are innumerable styles and many variations, but it is the setting or the interior which dictates the style. Another starting point can be answered by asking yourself what the flowers are for. If it is for the pleasure of looking at them in the home, then you can pick what you like or what you can spare, but if you wish to show your skill in the art of flower arranging to family or friends, then you will pick according to the needs of the design, and a more interesting design is always achieved by using different forms, shapes and sizes. This all brings the flower arranger to grow plants that will provide various shapes, sizes and colours.

I remember some years ago walking round Suttons trial grounds when my

eyes fell on a very light yellowy green flower. It was a *Nicotiana* but never before seen in that colour. 'What would you call it?' Mr. Sutton asked, and I replied that it must be 'Lime' or 'Lime Green', and I added that I loved it. It gave such a beautiful highlight to so many otherwise monotone arrangements and seemed to set a fashion for green flowers. In my Sussex garden I have a green border and I am sure many flower arrangers, like me, grow such green flowers as *Helleborus corsicus*, several euphorbias, *Alchemilla mollis* (lady's mantle) (I use this almost too much in the summer, for it is lovely), the lime green *Nicotiana*, *Tellima grandiflora*, *Amaranthus caudatus* 'Viridis' (green love-lies-bleeding), *Moluccella laevis* (Bells of Ireland) and the climber *Cobaea scandens*, though this turns purple as it matures. *Sedum* 'Autumn Joy' is another plant that is useful in its green stage for the centre of large arrangements and it looks good in modern designs. I remember I brought three stems of this up to London from my garden and placed them on a pinholder in a shallow dish, adding some stones low down to hide the holder, I kept them well watered and after some weeks, I noticed that roots had appeared. So here is an idea for some town dwellers. This plant gradually turns pink, then dull red; it even dried well.

Flowers that dry well are a further attraction to the flower arranger. Take the tall stems of acanthus for instance. They give architectural beauty in a perennial border, but when cut in late summer and hung upside down in a warm place to dry, will give height to many designs, whether of dry or fresh flowers. I use them a lot for Church decorations, leaving them in situ, adding fresh flowers as and when needed. The yellow achillea also dries well with no trouble as also does golden rod (*Solidago*). Many plants are grown specially for their drying qualities. Flowers such as the dainty pink acroclinium (*Helipterum*), statice (*Limonium*) and *Helichrysum bracteatum* are everlastings grown from seed and these can make lovely permanent decorations for a bedroom or hall. Ornamental grasses are also grown especially for indoor decoration. I love the nodding heads of quaking grass (*Briza*) and often sprinkle it with glitter at Christmas time.

Whilst it seems easy to have flowers in the house during summer, when the garden abounds with all varieties and colours, it is in the autumn that berries and seed heads come into their own. Shrubs such as *Viburnum opulus*, *Cotoneaster*, *Berberis* (various colours), *Pyracantha*, *Euonymus* and others all produce colourful berries, and if the sprays are covered with thin clear varnish or sprayed with hair lacquer, the berries will stay firm on the stems for a longer period than usual.

The art of flower arranging, because of the materials used, has brought many more thousands into the realm of gardening, proving, if proof were needed, that it is not only outside that flowers and plants are grown for pleasure but also for the inside where some of them will contribute to an overall artistic design. The gardener and the decorator do not always see eye to eye. I have often picked some leaves from the underside of a plant where they are turning yellow, only to be told by the gardener that he has some far better ones to offer, adding that the ones I had picked look sickly. They were just what I wanted for a certain colour scheme. We do not always want the straightest stems, or the biggest blooms; we like to see them in all stages of growth.

I have often referred to flower arranging as an end product of gardening. Even after the light has faded and the curtains are drawn, the pleasure can be extended by bringing some of the garden indoors.

Old Garden
Roses

Jack Harkness

Rosa gallica 'Camaieux'

IN THE course of the nineteenth century, a great divide separated the newly appearing roses from the old familiar ones. It was a consequence of the China Rose demonstrating its powerful influence as a marriage partner. Of course there had always been new roses and old roses. Before the divide, the new roses were very much like the old. After it, they were entirely different.

Not only were the new roses different, but in some respects very much better; as witness their brighter foliage and longer period in bloom. With all the attraction and interest aroused by novelty, to say nothing of its powerful, if often deceitful lure to optimism, the world in general took Teas and Noisettes, Bourbons and Hybrid Perpetuals to its heart, and looked upon the roses of former days as experiments discarded in the search for progress. This was good Darwinian and Victorian sense.

A few rosarians of the nineteenth century protested against the wholesale neglect of the old roses; they were of course right. It was not a case of which roses were better for a given purpose, but rather of preserving the exquisite variety of the genus. To keep the new and lose the old would be like assuming that because Mozart is the more popular, we might as well dump the works of Bach in the dustbin.

Those protesting voices in the nineteenth century raised but a lonely cry in the rose garden, altogether outshouted by the bustle of transport and rose shows and newly established rose nurseries from about 1870. The rose changed from being a flowering shrub into a florist's bloom, grown in roseries in decent seclusion so that its gauntness was shielded from the general view. And writers began to wonder why roses looked so miserable; as witness the words of T.W. Girdlestone in the *Rosarian's Year Book 1890*: 'the general effect produced by them in the garden is almost always incredibly poor'.

The remedy for Mr Girdlestone's troubles was introduced in the very year he aired his complaint. For I think we may take 'Mme Caroline Testout' as the rose above all others which taught the world that the rose could be a bedding plant. It was bright pink, with innocently rounded blooms, most regularly abiding to their typical form, appearing in multitudes at an even height; and performing thus twice or oftener in a season. The era of the Hybrid Tea rose was now in being.

From that point, roses jumped over the rambler-clad fences of their se-cluded roseries, began to elbow geraniums out of their well-sited beds, and invaded the prime points of the garden. It was a two-pronged attack, the army of Hybrid Teas being reinforced by Polyantha roses, whose intended special purpose was to be bedding plants; and in due course, the two armies mingled, with the result of Floribundas, and an even more distant retreat by annuals and herbaceous plants.

It is not unfair to say that if during the 1940s or 1950s, one had taken the question of preserving old roses around most of the best-known rosarians, the answers would have ranged from incredulity to mockery. 'Would you', the experts liked to ask in their confident way, 'exchange your motor car for a horse and trap?'

And the dreamy look of longing which rose to the eyes upon that divine prospect being envisaged was accounted by the experts as a conversion to their sensible view.

While suburbia was being crammed with modern roses, a few crackpots were obstinately specializing in old ones. Looking back, it would seem that the chain was fragile indeed. There were still some nurserymen who grew the old cultivars, most especially Edward Bunyard of Maidstone in Kent. He seems to be very nearly solely responsible in Britain for passing on the knowledge of the past into our generation. His *Old Garden Roses* was published in 1936. Hunt through the rose literature of the previous years, and the nearest links with Bunyard one finds are Rivers and Paul, about a century earlier.

Bunyard had an important collection of old roses; and another existed in Hertfordshire, in the nurseries of G. Beckwith & Son of Hoddesdon. I have heard the supposition, but lack the evidence for it, that their collection was founded on that of Paul & Son. At all events, it was the Beckwith collection that was bought by Thomas Hilling, and became the particular study of Graham Thomas, whom we may take to be the successor of Edward Bunyard. He soon found other sources of old roses in various gardens about the land, eventually issued his remarkable *Manual of Shrub Roses*, and safely put the knowledge of the old roses into the minds of folk now living.

Thus, perilously, were the old roses conveyed into our hands. To see what they were up against, read this passage from the *Rose Annual 1950*: 'It may be worthwhile repeating here the result of an attempt to make an "Old Rose" garden in this district about twelve years ago. The work was done by a person who claimed to be an authority on old Roses. A very good site was selected and no expense spared in preparation. £200 was spent on Roses, which at that time cost about 1/6 each. English and Continental nurseries were well combed and varieties from every known section were purchased. The result was a bitter disappointment to all concerned. The same garden had a lovely lot of more modern roses in another part, and to go from this to the old Roses was like going from the sublime to the ridiculous. Even the most prejudiced die-hard old Rose "fan" could not have found much more than a morbid interest in it. I felt like passing through the garden at funeral pace with cap in hand and head bowed, for never had I beheld anything so tragic . . . Have your Madame Tussauds and British Rose Museums if you wish, Chelsea Show is good enough for me.'

For most readers of the *Rose Annual*, that put the eccentrics who praised old roses firmly in their place.

The study and preservation of old roses occurred not only in Britain, but in varying degree wherever serious rosarians were to be found, especially in France, Germany, Switzerland and the United States.

Let us now look across the great divide, and see what were those old roses left on the far side of it.

They were the classes known as Gallicas, Damasks, Albas and Centifolias. Of these, the Centifolias were comparative youngsters, going back only to the sixteenth century. The other three are archetypal roses of the Western world, covering so far as we can tell the whole span of our recorded history. This claim is not made for individual cultivars, for the chances are that these have changed over the generations. It is the types which can reasonably be assumed to have remained more or less constant, giving rise to the belief that when one of these roses is plucked to-day, it would have looked as familiar to Shakespeare, to Charlemagne and to Cleopatra, as it does to us.

If indeed there is such a community of experience through the ages to be established, then the old roses were wisely preserved.

Rosa chinensis var. minima

The Gallicas were probably the earliest of all, as having risen directly from the wild rose *R. gallica*, which grows across Central Europe into Western Asia. In its true wild form, *R. gallica* has single pink flowers, fairly large for a wild rose, and pretty. Fortunately it produced many variations from its true form, particularly in colour and in doubleness. Upon being brought into cultivation and propagated, the variations in time gave rise to still more, so that a whole range of Gallica cultivars came into being.

R. gallica is a fairly low-growing, sprawling shrub, with soft green leaves. It flowers around midsummer in Britain. It has very few thorns but many bristles, very closely set. From it came the red roses of the West, of which the earliest example known is *R. gallica officinalis*.

Few roses have so many names as this one. The most sensible is 'The Red Rose', which appears in the earliest English list of roses by John Gerard in 1597. From that to the 'Red Rose of Lancaster' is but a step, although we may assume that the Lancasters' emblem was heraldic rather than botanic and that any red rose would have done for them. Due to its uses in medicine, this rose was known as the 'Apothecary's Rose'; and because various tonics were made from it as a speciality by the people of Provins, it bore the name of that town too, as the 'Provins Rose'. It was also known in England as 'Red Damask', a most unfortunate error, for it is pure Gallica and not Damask at all.

This cheerful, semi-double rose gave rise to a remarkable striped sport, in which the red is divided down the petal length by bands of blush pink. A striped rose was described in Europe in 1581, and therefore presumably existed long before that date; however the one we have to-day, *R. gallica* 'Versicolor', has a date ascribed to it of about 1650; it enjoys the name 'Rosa Mundi', and is surely one of the most paintable and photogenic of roses.

The trouble with these old roses was always their brief period in flower. People think none the worse of rhododendrons and flowering cherries on that account, but they cannot bear that the roses should fade. Writing in 1832, Thomas Rivers suggested that to prolong the flowering period 'two plants of each variety should be planted; one plant to be pruned in October and the other in May'.

Out of Gerard's *Herball, or Generall Historie of Plantes* in 1597, we can pluck 'The Velvet Rose'. This was 'of a deepe and blacke red colour, resembling red crimson velvet'. One can imagine the attraction of the word velvet in describing the pile on a rose petal, and conveying an impression of richness and beauty. It led to quite a number of velvet roses being catalogued. However we still have one which is possibly the same as Gerard's; or if not, it is very similar to it. This is 'Tuscany', a more upright grower than most Gallicas, with very fine semi-double flowers in darkest red, the stamens alight in the darkness.

If 'Tuscany' is indeed 'The Velvet Rose', then it prompts the thought that it came from Italy; and may possibly have a long story to tell before 1597.

The other Gallicas grown to-day have originated in the eighteenth or nineteenth centuries. One could fairly easily obtain about 50 cultivars; in *The Rose Garden*, written in 1848, William Paul listed 471. Some well-known sorts are 'Belle de Crécy', 'Camaieux', 'Cardinal de Richelieu', 'Charles de Mills', 'Perle des Panachées', 'Président de Sèze' and 'Tricolore de Flandres'.

How the Gallicas turned into Damasks is one of time's secrets. There are affinities to be seen in the leaves, and the petals; but not in the growth. Where the Gallicas live in a low, lax but compact way, the Damasks lift themselves higher and very often arch out as open shrubs. For this tendency, the usual explanation is that a climbing rose must have married *R. gallica*; and because the Damasks are exceedingly fragrant, a fragrant climber is postulated. There are two candidates, *R. phoenicea*, a Middle Eastern species, and the Musk Rose, *R. moschata*, which probably came from further east long, long ago.

How and when the Damasks were born remains a mystery, but one thing is sure, that they have supplied the fragrance of roses to perfumeries for a long time. This is indeed the first recorded use of roses; and it is still practised, particularly in the Valley of Roses in Bulgaria, where *R.* × *damascena* 'Trigintipetala' is the chief cultivar used to supply attar of roses. The Bulgarian industry was almost certainly implanted by the Turks, when Bulgaria was part of the Ottoman Empire. From whom the Turks learned to use a Damask rose, and for how long they had it, are two questions with no answer.

Among the Damasks was a remarkable cultivar called 'Quatre Saisons'. Remarkable for being an old rose which flowered twice in the season, it earned the exaggerated name 'Four Seasons'; the modest Latin one *R. bifera*, or 'twice-bearing'; which was outdone by the supplanting *R.* × *damascena* 'Semperflorens', or 'ever-blooming Damask'; it was perhaps most sensibly described by the English name which hit on its outstanding character: 'Autumn Damask'.

This is a double pink rose, of unknown age; the one certain thing about it is that rosarians of old were never liable to part with their one remontant rose.

The most beautiful Damask is the white 'Madame Hardy', introduced in 1832. The most famous is the 'York and Lancaster Rose', *R.* × *damascena* 'Versicolor', from which in Shakespeare's *Henry VI* the roses of different colours were picked: red and white, in popular imagining; but in Shakespeare 'blushing shame', 'white despair' and a third 'stolen of both'. Such indeed is the somewhat anaemic appearance of this famous rose.

One could find about twenty Damasks to-day; William Paul in 1848 listed 201 of various sorts. Some of the other survivors are 'Celsiana', 'La Ville de Bruxelles', 'Léda' (the Painted Damask) and 'Marie Louise'.

The third grand original class of roses is the Albas. These are stalwart plants, large and upright, full of handsome leaf. The flowers appear about midsummer, in very pretty double forms, generally pale pink or white in colour. These roses are particularly hardy and long-lived.

Their origin, according to C.C. Hurst, was most probably from the marriage of a smooth-wooded species of the dog rose section and a Damask. He credits the ancient Greeks and Romans with growing them, and traces mention of them in writings of the thirteenth, fourteenth and fifteenth centuries. However, the identity of plants in writings of those times is unprovable. Let us be content with saying the class is very old.

Albas are most beautiful shrub roses, as anyone may prove by planting 'Celestial', 'Félicité Parmentier', 'Mme Legras de St Germain' or 'Maiden's Blush'. The delicate blush colouring of 'Celestial' is one of nature's best works of art.

If one forgets the preconceived idea of a rose, learned from looking at Hybrid Teas, and opens one's eyes to the intricate petallage of Albas, many a beauty lies ready to be enjoyed. 'Celestial', for example, has about 25 small petals, but those at the centre are narrow, and admit a view of the stamens; in 'Maiden's Blush', the stamens are hidden a longer time by the central petals folding over them. 'Mme Legras de St Germain' is snowy white, and opens with the centre like a little snowball, the outer petals stretched around it. Then the central petals arise, starting at the outside of the snowball, each one standing up straight, folded down its middle, the whole like a little powder puff.

'Félicité Parmentier' is even more charming, for when its 'snowball' at the centre begins to part, it is seen to be pink within; the petals have white outside and pink inside, and a pretty blushing confusion they create.

'Maiden's Blush' is an old cultivar and tempted the French into many loving, lustful names, among them 'La Virginale', La Séduisante', 'Incarnata' and 'Cuisse de Nymphe', which means 'Maiden's Thigh'.

An extremely vigorous Alba is 'Semi-plena'. This one bears a fine crop of hips, which the double ones do not have. It is sometimes sold as 'Bonnie Prince Charlie's Rose'.

William Paul listed 61 Albas in 1848. One could hope to find about twelve nowadays, including two which have more hybrid character than those already mentioned. They are 'Königin von Danemarck' and 'Pompon Blanc Parfait'.

Last of the four classes of true Old Garden Roses is the Centifolias. They were last in point of time, as having been raised in the sixteenth century, we may hope a thousand and more years later than the others.

There is plenty of doubt to cloud them even so, as regards their parents, their place of origin and their name. Alas that no Rose Societies published Annuals in those days!

The parents, according to C.C. Hurst, were most likely to have been the Autumn Damask and an Alba. However it would be interesting to hear a debate between two well-informed rosarians as to whether Autumn Damask and Gallica were not more likely.

Their place of origin is reflected in two names which John Gerard gave in 1597, when he called this the 'Holland or Province Rose'. It is assumed that the class was raised in Holland, and widely grown in the South of France, or particularly in Provence, by our spelling.

The name was still further confused by the use of the word Centifolia. This was taken from the references to the 'Hundred-petalled Rose' by Theophrastus in ancient Greece, and Pliny in ancient Rome. And within a short time, many people convinced themselves that here was the same rose the ancients grew.

The English began to call it the Cabbage Rose. This may have been because they spent much of their time fighting either the Dutch or the French, and wanted no reminder of their enemies among their roses. The name was descriptive of the way the petals were wrapped in a tight ball at the heart of the flower, like a round cabbage in all but size. A Centifolia rose has quite a small flower; but thanks to being called a Cabbage Rose, it got the reputation of possessing an enormous bloom, and must have disappointed many a puzzled purchaser.

About the year 1700, the Centifolias gave rise to a sport destined to be greatly loved. This was the Moss rose, in which the calyx and ovary bear little green mossy fronds or bristles. The best is 'Common Moss', which is pink, and possibly the original sport. Many other Moss roses are not so pleasantly mossed as they should be.

Among the famous Centifolias are 'Bullata', 'Chapeau de Napoléon', which has strange long fronds upon its sepals, so that its buds do indeed look as if they wear that famous headgear; 'De Meaux', 'Petite de Hollande', 'Spong' and 'Tour de Malakoff'. And of the Moss roses, 'Comtesse de Murinais', 'Blanche Moreau', 'Capitaine John Ingram', 'Nuits de Young' and 'William Lobb' are pre-eminent.

In 1848, William Paul recorded 76 Centifolias and 84 Moss roses, total 160. One could hope to find to-day fairly easily about eighteen Centifolias and 30 Mosses, total 48.

Such were the roses of the antique Western world, before the invader from China transmuted them by the touch of its golden pollen. They are neither better nor worse than modern roses, only different. They fit a different concept of gardening, and by no means challenge 'Iceberg' or 'Allgold' for their beds.

Let us hope that when the next great divide occurs, somebody in the future will save the Floribundas and Hybrid Teas from extinction in their turn.

Decorative Climbing Plants

Noël J. Prockter, F.L.S.

Clematis montana

T ODAY there are climbers and wall shrubs which can be used in a variety of situations whether a garden is large, medium or small. Even a flat-dweller can grow a clematis, ivy or Chilean glory flower (*Eccremocarpus scaber*) in a tub where space permits. There is usually a fence, wall or trellis that will benefit from some kind of climber and there are climbers that need the protection of a wall or fence, such as *Lapageria rosea*.

In larger or medium-sized gardens climbers can be used most effectively to clamber through the branches of an old apple tree, for example *Wisteria sinensis*, *Clematis montana*, roses such as *Rosa filipes* 'Kiftsgate', *R. longicuspis* and *R.* × 'Wedding Day'; even though the last two roses are known as ramblers, they still clamber in and over trees.

Whether an archway, trellis or wires on a wall, make sure that supports for climbers are strong and secure. Wooden posts should be at least 4 in. (10 cm) in diameter, brick pillars 9 in. (23 cm) in diameter. Posts need to be set in the ground to a depth of 18 in. (45 cm). Wooden structures should be treated with a wood preservative to prevent rotting.

Sometimes it is necessary to increase the height of a dividing wall or fence. This can be achieved by fixing a trellis or posts and wires above the top of a wall or fence. The training of a climber is then an easy operation. Where light is important during the winter months, choose deciduous climbers such as clematis or wisteria so that after a frost the foliage falls.

A useful and attractive method of growing climbers is to train them to a tripod of three posts fixed at the top. Alternatively, use a tree trunk, ideally a conifer such as spruce, for this purpose.

When growing climbers against a wall or fence plant them at least 9 to 12 in. (23 to 30 cm) away from its support; this then enables rain to reach the soil around the base of the plant. Where plants attach themselves to a wall by means of aerial roots (ivy) or disks at the end of tendrils (Virginia creeper), it is still necessary to set the climber away from a wall or fence. Simply push in a small supporting cane to lead the main shoot to where it is going to cling.

There are on the market today various types of supports to attach to walls and fences. But first there are those wrought iron galvanized 'vine eyes' through which wires can be strained and secured. Horizontal wires should be spaced at least 9 in. (23 cm) apart and supported by 6 in. (15 cm) 'eyes', spacing these 6 ft (2 m) apart. Ready-made supports such as Netlon's Garden Mesh, Climbing Plant Supports and Clematis Supports can now be had from garden centres and shops. For tying climbers to their supports I always use plain fillis – or green can be used if preferred.

Before planting make sure that the ground is well dug and that the soil is well moistened: such advice is of paramount importance. A useful method to ensure that moisture reaches the roots of climbers, especially those planted near a wall or fence, is to sink a drain pipe where water can be poured. When water has to be applied, always give a good soaking to the ground, then follow with a mulch of well-rotted manure, peat or rotted garden compost;

this will cut down the work of watering so frequently.

Tender plants may require some form of protection at first until they become fully established. This I did with a plant of *Abutilon megapotamicum* (strictly a wall shrub, but grown as a climber); for the first year or so I placed dry bracken around the base of the plant, which repaid me handsomely in future years.

A point to remember with clematis is that they enjoy a cool root run, so if the plant is placed in full sun a slab of stone in front of the plant will protect it from the sun. Alternatively plant a small shrub such as lavender, rosemary or rue (*Ruta graveolens* 'Jackman's Blue'). Never forget that a newly planted climber must first make new roots and become established before it starts to climb, cling or twine.

I suppose most of us enthuse about the plants that we find most attractive. A wall shrub I never tire of is *Abutilon megapotamicum* and its variegated form *A. m.* 'Variegatum'; both are charming and intriguing plants because of their chinese-lantern-like flowers which are made up of a red calyx with yellow petals from which protrude brown anthers; the flowers are freely borne on wiry shoots. What suits them best is a warm south or west wall or fence and if trained on wires or trellis they will make a spectacular show from late April to early May right through to late autumn or early winter in favoured localities. In my previous garden in Sussex my plant was still flowering in November 1978. It is necessary to cut back any frosted shoots or weak shoots in spring.

An interesting tendril climber is the Chilean glory flower, *Eccremocarpus scaber*; this is a semi-woody almost evergreen climber, not fully hardy in cold districts. Again in Sussex, I had a plant which grew satisfactorily for three or four years against a west-facing wall. The pretty, tubular, orange-scarlet and orange-yellow flowers, each about 1 in. (2.5 cm) long, are carried on graceful 6 to 10 in. (15 to 25 cm) long racemes bearing ten to twenty flowers. It is frequently grown as an annual and as such, seed should be sown in February in gentle heat, the seedlings potted on and finally planted out-of-doors in May. Established plants will often start flowering in April, continuing until spoiled by frost in late autumn. Any soil suits eccremocarpus except a thin chalky one.

Pruning can be done in March or April, when dead or frosted growth should be cut back and one or two main shoots cut back fairly hard to encourage new growth near the base.

What a disappointment wisterias can be. I have known of cases where plants have been growing for almost twenty years and hardly produced a flower. At least part of the answer to this conundrum is that the plant had been raised from seed. Therefore make sure your plant has been vegetatively propagated from a free-flowering stock. To this the final answer is: always buy from a reliable nurseryman.

Another reason for lack of flower from even a vegetatively propagated wisteria is that correct pruning has not been carried out. To encourage plenty of flower buds, pinch out the tips of young lateral shoots when they have made four to five leaves, doing this four or five times during the summer. In winter when all the foliage is off, cut back all laterals to within two or three buds; at the same time leave any shoots which are required to extend the plant further, otherwise cut such shoots back. Wisterias like good living, so before planting incorporate well-rotted manure or garden compost and bone meal at the rate of 4 oz per sq. yd.

Lapageria rosea

An interesting and rather unusual twining shrubby climber is *Actinidia kolomikta*; this has tri-coloured variegated leaves, which in spring are a striking metallic green, but are even more striking during the summer when the leaves become suffused with pink and white. To obtain good variegated foliage, plant against a south or west wall in full sun. Height up to 20 ft (6 m).

A pretty semi-evergreen twiner is *Akebia quinata*, each leaf stalk usually having five leaflets (hence its name *quinata*). In April and May fragrant flowers are produced with the new leaves; each cluster has several tiny pale purple male flowers and a few large chocolate-purple female ones up to $1\frac{1}{2}$ in. (4 cm) wide: an intriguing arrangement. It is an ideal plant for a wall, trellis or pergola, and is happiest in an acid or loamy soil. Height 30 to 40 ft (9 to 12 m). The flowers are followed by purplish sausage-like fruits up to 4 in. (10 cm) long. The allied *A. trifoliata*, usually deciduous, is an elegant climber with three leaflets to each leaf stalk, and produces deep purple flowers in spring.

All too often gardeners are confronted with a wall or fence which is shaded. In such an instance I would choose that unusual and beautiful evergreen from Chile, *Berberidopsis corallina*, introduced over a century ago (1862) but still not seen anything like enough. The first time I remember seeing a plant in flower was in 1935, as a student at Kew; its globose crimson-red flowers were hanging among the dark green leathery leaves, which are glaucous beneath. This semi-twining climber needs wall support and protection from north and east winds. A south- or west-facing wall where there is shade from nearby trees or shrubs is the ideal position. Avoid strongly limy soils and add plenty of leaf mould to thin sandy ones. An acid loamy soil suits it best. Height 6 to 10 ft (2 to 3 m). No regular pruning should be necessary. If it has to be pruned, do this either in spring or after flowering.

Few gardens will be without a clematis – after all, if one so wishes, it is possible to have beauty from species or cultivars throughout the year. The first to flower is *Clematis cirrhosa*. Above its evergreen foliage, nodding creamy-white flowers, red-freckled inside, are produced in January or February. Then there is *C. armandii* 'Snowdrift', bearing huge clusters of white flowers at the end of March to April. Recently in a friend's garden I saw a plant of this clematis clambering through an old specimen tree of *Prunus* 'Pissardii'; a most effective combination.

Two beauties that bloom in May are *C. macropetala* 'Lagoon', having semi-double, deep lavender nodding flowers, with pointed petals. Equally lovely is *C. montana* 'Elizabeth', a beautiful pink-flowered cultivar having larger, long-stemmed flowers which are sweetly scented. From May into June the large-flowered hybrid 'Barbara Dibley' produces rich violet flowers with purple bars in the centre of each sepal. Dear old 'Nelly Moser' in the same group is too well known to need further description. Another large-flowered clematis is 'Elsa Spath', a vigorous grower having bright blue flowers, free-flowering from May to June.

My favourite white-flowered clematis is 'Marie Boisselot' ('Mme Le

Coultre'). It has shapely blossoms with broad rounded overlapping sepals set off by a boss of yellow stamens. 'William Kennett' has large lavender-mauve flowers with crimped edges to the sepals, each being ribbed down the centre. This magnificent flower, with brown stamens, blooms from June to July. Another favourite is 'Comtesse de Bouchard', having charming saucer-shaped, soft pink flowers with a tint of mauve. It is free-flowering from June to October.

Two cultivars of C. *viticella* are 'Ernest Markham', having petunia-red flowers with a velvety sheen. It is eventually free-flowering, but I have found it requires a little patience before this happens. To encourage flowers, pinch out the tips of young shoots when they are about 3 ft (0.9 m) long. The other is 'Etoile Violette', having deep violet medium-sized flowers with yellow stamens; it is lavish with its blooms from June to August. At one time I had this clematis climbing up an old apple tree along with the rose 'Zéphirine Drouhin'. This Bourbon climbing rose with its exquisite bright carmine-pink, richly scented blooms made a spectacular display with the deep violet flowers of the clematis. The rose is of the old-fashioned type, and flowers freely on thornless stems from June to July and afterwards intermittently throughout the summer, Height 10 to 15 ft (3.0 to 4.5 m).

We all have our favourite roses; one of mine is 'Mme Grégoire Staechelin'. This large-flowered climber has coral-pink hybrid-tea-type blooms splashed with carmine on the outside. It flowers from late May into early July. The flowers are followed by large hips which at first are green, later in autumn orange-coloured, lasting all through the winter. Seen cascading from a high wall, this is a truly beautiful rose, richly scented, vigorous, free of mildew, and with large dark glossy green foliage which remains almost throughout the winter.

When a repeat-flowering climber is wanted, plant 'Pink Perpétue'; this *kordesii* climber has clusters of good-sized double blooms of clear pink with carmine-pink reverse.

Another large-flowered climbing rose is 'Golden Showers', having hybrid-tea-type clusters of long pointed buds opening to semi-double blooms of clear golden yellow. It is perpetual-flowering, fragrant and moderately vigorous. And yet another is 'Maigold', having deep buff-yellow flowers with golden stamens, repeat-flowering, richly scented, and stems covered with spiteful thorns.

To grow up and over tall trees, *Rosa filipes* 'Kiftsgate' cannot be bettered. In July it produces clouds of creamy-white fragrant flowers, each 1½ in. (4 cm) wide. In autumn it has red hips. 'Wedding Day' is a less vigorous rambler, having large trusses of very fragrant flowers, yellow in bud, opening to creamy-white, with bright orange stamens. Rich glossy green foliage completes the picture. Height up to 35 ft (10 m). At least as vigorous as *R. filipes*, and ideal for scrambling through trees, is *R. longicuspis*, which produces masses of single white flowers with a banana-like fragrance.

Another climber suitable for scrambling over trees is the hardy deciduous, vigorous twining climber *Celastrus orbiculatus*. It can however also be grown against a wall or fence, where its spectacular fruits can be shown off to advantage. The green flowers are small and insignificant, but in autumn it comes into its own, when the orange-yellow fruit capsules are fully ripe and split open into three, displaying bright seed coats during November, December and January. An added asset is the foliage, which turns to a clear yellow and enhances the bright fruits. It is one of those climbers that is not fussy over soils. If pruning is necessary to restrict growth, cut back any unwanted shoots, also any weak ones, in February.

Three spectacular creepers for south or west walls belong to the genus *Campsis*. First there is the scandent climber or twiner *C. grandiflora* (*C. chinensis*). Among the long pinnate leaves, made up of seven to nine leaflets, are borne panicles of six to nine large orange-scarlet trumpets, as much as 3 in. (8 cm) wide at the mouth. I have seen plants covering a south-facing house wall reaching well up to the gutter. The trumpet vine, *C. radicans*, is ideal for climbing through trees which it does by aerial roots in the same way as ivy. Combined with *Hydrangea petiolaris* it could make a spectacular display, the trumpet-shaped orange-coloured flowers, borne in clusters of four to twelve, but only 1½ in. (4 cm) across, mingling with the large flat white flower clusters of the hydrangea – not that I have ever seen this done. The last of this trio is *C.* × *tagliabuana* 'Madame Galen', a hybrid between the above two campsis. It has vivid salmon-red trumpets carried in shorter crowded panicles.

Although more usually grown as a half-hardy annual, the 'Jack and the beanstalk' or 'cup and saucer' creeper *Cobaea scandens* should not be neglected as a rapid coverer of walls and sheds. It gets its name from the Canterbury-bell-like flowers set in a saucer-like calyx. At first the flowers are green, changing to violet before finally falling and producing large acorn-shaped fruits. Our two sons named it the drain-pipe flower as the first time I grew some plants they very soon covered a drain pipe and reached up to a gutter on our fairly tall house. It is frost-tender and must not be planted out until early June. As for pruning, the first hard frost in autumn will do this for you. Plants are readily raised from seed sown in gentle heat.

What a teasing and frustrating climber the 'flame flower' *Tropaeolum speciosum* can be! Three times did I try in my garden when I lived in Sussex: the third time it grew but was not a howling success. The roots are rather like those of bindweed or bellbine. In Scotland I have seen it flourishing in hedges, making them come alight with the widely expanded scarlet nasturtium flowers. The ideal situation is where it can enjoy a cool root run and have a moist leafy soil in which to roam. According to William Robinson in *The English Flower Garden* 'No pains should be spared to establish this plant in a vigorous condition . . . the soil should be made light, and deep, and free by the addition of leaf-mould, peat, fibry loam, and sand, as the nature of the ground may require, and the surface should be mulched in summer with an inch or two or decomposed manure or leaf-mould to prevent excessive evaporation; but whatever kind of manure is used; it must be well decayed'. With this kindly advice I must try again in Hampshire, so here's hoping!

Fuchsias

Percy Thrower, V.M.H., N.D.H.

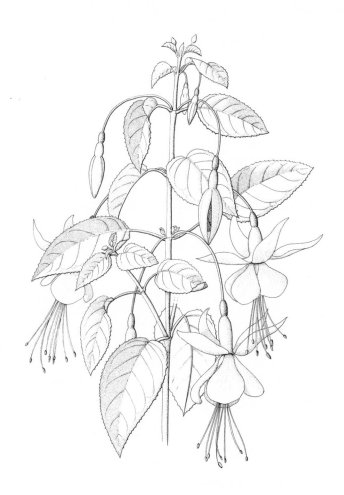

'Display'

T HE FUCHSIA is a great favourite of mine and one of our most versatile plants: it has so many uses, it is comparatively easy to grow, ideal for the greenhouse, sun lounge or conservatory, and can be had in flower over a very long period, from April to November. There are a large number of cultivars and a wide range of colours; there are the half-hardy sorts which need to be kept safe from frost during the winter months, and the hardy varieties which can be left in the garden from year to year.

My first love for fuchsias began many years ago when I was a mere lad starting my gardening career under my father. A head gardener on a large private estate in Buckinghamshire, father prided himself on growing large standard fuchsias in tubs and urns on a broad terrace in front of the mansion. I then moved to the Royal Gardens at Windsor to further my training in horticulture, and there was a sight I shall always remember, a plant corridor some 400 yards long which connected the various growing and display greenhouses. This corridor had fuchsias trained up and over the roof on either side and it was a wonderful spectacle to see the flowers in many colours hanging from the branches. Those fuchsias were very many years old at that time and included many of the cultivars which are still popular at the present time. From Windsor to public parks in first Leeds, then Derby and then Shrewsbury, and I found fuchsias of immense value for greenhouse display, bedding and many other uses. I moved from Derby to Shrewsbury in January 1946, in the days of 'Dig for Victory', when there were restrictions on the use of heat for non-edible crops. In one of the greenhouses at Shrewsbury there were some 50-odd plants of various sorts of fuchsia and I decided in my first year as Parks Superintendent it was essential to make a good display in the parks and gardens. As there were already the stock plants in the greenhouse, fuchsias would be used to form the main part of the many displays in the various parts of the town. Shrewsbury is an old mediaeval town and I could see fuchsias fitting in well with the old stone and the black and white buildings. I began by propagating every shoot that was available on the 50-odd plants, and every shoot thereafter as it was produced. As the cuttings rooted and formed their growth, the tops of each one of these were taken and rooted in the propagating frame, and again the tops of these were taken when the plants had formed four or five pairs of leaves, and so it continued. By the end of May in that first year when planting time came I had more than 5,000 fuchsia plants at my disposal for beds and borders, tubs in various parts of the town, in window-boxes and in hanging baskets in the old buildings. The fuchsias did fit in to the surroundings as I thought they would do. I still grow many thousands of fuchsia plants in more than 60 different cultivars.

The fuchsia makes one of the best of all standard flowering plants, 120 cm (4 ft) or more tall to provide extra height and colour in bedding schemes, to be grown in tubs or other containers or as specimen plants in the greenhouse or conservatory. It makes a fine bush plant for pots or for planting out in beds and borders. It will be gathered from what I have already said that it is ideal for window-boxes and for hanging baskets, and as a window-sill plant in the house provided it is kept in the maximum amount of light. In the majority of our larger flower shows, beginning with the Chelsea Flower Show in May, the fuchsia now takes pride of place. We see many fine large exhibits staged by professional growers, and fine specimen plants exhibited by the amateurs.

Propagation

The fuchsia is among the easiest of plants to propagate from cuttings and these can be taken at any time from February to October. Young shoots 5 to 10 cm (2 to 4 in.) long make the ideal cuttings and during most of the year it will be impossible to find non-flowering shoots to make into cuttings, but this makes very little difference. If flowers and buds are removed from the shoots, we still have good cuttings. To make the cuttings with a sharp knife or an old razor blade, cut straight across immediately below the lower pair of leaves, remove the lower leaves so that there is an inch or so of clean stem. Dip the base of each cutting first into water and then into a hormone rooting powder; this speeds up the rooting process and prevents many failures. There are various rooting media that can be used: John Innes Seed Sowing Compost, all-peat growing composts, Vermiculite and similar materials, and peat and sand mixed together in equal parts. I must say I prefer a mixture of peat and coarse sand in equal parts and find this the most successful. The cuttings can be put into pots or into boxes and it is essential to label each cultivar carefully. As a matter of interest, it is also worth putting the date on the label. When inserting the cuttings into the peat and sand mixture in the pots or boxes it is essential to ensure that the base of the cuttings reaches the bottom of the holes made with the dibber and that the peat and sand is pressed lightly in, so that the part of the stem below the peat and sand is in complete contact and not in an air space. There is an old gardening term that cuttings are sometimes 'hanged'; this means the base of the cutting is in an air space or pocket at the bottom of the hole made by the dibber instead of being in close contact with the peat-and-sand mixture. The result then is that the cutting flags and may eventually die or take a long time before it will form its roots.

After putting the cuttings into the pots or boxes, stand them aside and give them a thorough watering. When the surplus water has drained away they can then go into a close propagating frame where a minimum temperature of 15-18°C (60-65°F) can be maintained. The object of a propagating frame where the atmosphere can be kept close and humid is to prevent loss of moisture from the leaves and the flagging of the cuttings, and it will be necessary to shade them from the sun during the warmest part of the day. Under these conditions the cuttings should have formed a good root system in three to four weeks and be ready to come out of the frame and to be placed on the greenhouse staging for a few days before being potted separately into small pots.

Potting

For potting the cuttings an all-peat growing compost can be used or the John Innes Potting Compost No. 1. The young plants will form new roots and grow faster in the all-peat growing medium than in the John Innes No. 1, but the plants will not be so well balanced nor as sturdy. Sometimes it is impossible these days to get good-quality John Innes composts, and in this case I would recommend using the all-peat composts. After potting the plants must be thoroughly watered in and it will be necessary to shade them from the sun for the first few days, until they begin to get established in the new compost. Sheets of newspaper lightly placed over the plants is an economical means of shading. Potting on into larger pots is done as the plants become well established in their present pots; when roots begin to appear through the drainage holes in the base of the pots it is a fair indication that they are ready to be moved on into larger pots. The principle from the beginning must be to grow large plants in small pots and not small plants in large pots. Flowerpots 9 cm (3½ in.) in diameter are the ideal for the first potting. When ready for moving the plants on, a 13 cm (5 in.) diameter pot is then large enough, and eventually into a 18 cm (7 in.) diameter container. Few small-greenhouse owners will want the plants in anything larger. The John Innes Potting Composts No.s 2 or 3 are perhaps the best, if a good sample is available.

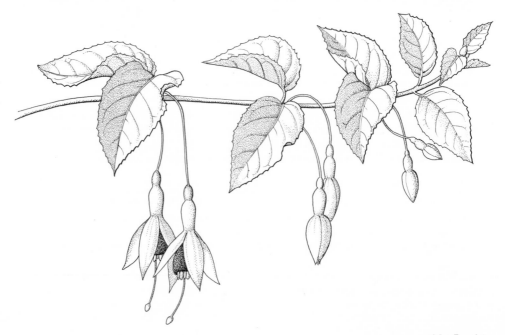

'Mrs Popple'

Training

It must be decided in the early stages what kind of plant it is intended to grow: bush, standard, half-standard, or trailing for a window-box or hanging basket. A 5 to 10 cm (2 to 4 in.) cutting taken in August or September can be grown into a good standard plant 120 cm (4 ft) or more high which will be in full flower by late May of the following year. To do this of course means keeping the plant growing throughout the winter in a minimum temperature of 10°C (50°F). After potting the rooted cutting into a 9 cm (3½ in.) pot, provide the young plant with a cane and fasten it to this support as it grows upwards. Pinch the tip from each side shoot as it grows at the first pair of leaves; leaving this one pair of leaves on the side shoots helps to strengthen the stem of the standard plant. When the plant has reached the required height (90 to 120 cm (3 to 4 ft) or more), pinch out the young growing tip. Side shoots which will grow from the three to four leaf joints at the top of the plant should be allowed to grow until they have formed five or six pairs of leaves, and then have their tips removed. This is to promote branches to form the head of the standard. More side shoots will grow from these, and again the tips can be pinched at the fifth pair of leaves to ensure a really bushy head to the standard. A half-standard, 75 to 90 cm (2½ to 3 ft) high, is treated in exactly the same way, the growing tip being pinched out when it has reached the required height. There are some cultivars of fuchsias more suited for growing as standard plants than others; others are more suited for growing as bush plants and there are those more suited for hanging baskets and window boxes, but I will deal with that later.

To form a good specimen bush, allow the young plant to form six or seven pairs of leaves and then pinch out the growing tip. Side branches will form as a result of this stopping, and these should be allowed to form six or seven pairs of leaves before the tips of each of these is pinched out. After this stage the plant can be allowed to produce its flowers, which it will do freely, or if a large specimen plant is required, pinch out the young tips of each of the young branches again.

Trailing fuchsias for hanging baskets or for a similar use can be 'stopped' or, to put it more plainly, the young tip can be pinched out at the fifth or sixth pair of leaves and the tips from the side shoots at the fifth or sixth pair of leaves. When growing these in a hanging basket I continue to pinch the tips from the young branches until the basket itself is completely covered by the plant.

Planting

The half-hardy types of fuchsias must not be planted outside, and neither must hanging baskets be hung outside until late May or early June when the fear of frosts has gone. Bush plants which hold their flowers up, and some varieties do more than others, can be planted in beds and borders to good effect. Tubs or other containers on the patio or terrace planted with a standard or half-standard plant in the centre and bush plants planted around make a very attractive feature, and with regular watering and feeding can be counted on to flower from June to October without fail. For planting in tubs and other containers I prefer to use the John Innes Potting Compost No. 3. In hanging baskets and window-boxes they will flower continuously too if they receive regular attention in the way of watering and feeding.

When planting standard plants in beds or borders to provide height and colour between other bedding plants I prefer to leave a saucer-like depression around the stem of each plant to make watering and feeding that much easier. They will need a strong stake, such as a 2.5 × 2.5 cm (1 × 1 in.) dahlia or rose stake, to support the plants against strong winds.

Those fuchsias planted in tubs or similar containers on a patio or terrace, once well established, will require watering every day, rain or no rain, and on warm sunny days twice a day. The fuchsia is a plant which responds to good treatment, perhaps better than any other, and feeding twice a week by adding liquid fertilizer to the water will keep it growing and flowering continuously.

Hanging Baskets

The fuchsia is, I consider, the finest of all plants for making a good and colourful hanging basket, and I prefer to plant baskets entirely with fuchsias rather than mix them with trailing lobelias, petunias or other plants. To allow time for the plants to make sufficient growth, it is essential to plant the baskets between late February and early April. Four plants is sufficient to make a good 40 cm (16 in.) diameter basket and three sufficient for a 35 cm (14 in.) basket. I would not recommend planting fuchsias in smaller baskets than these.

The baskets should firstly be lined with moss, such as can be found under hedgerows and in woodland areas or purchased from garden centres and garden shops, etc. The baskets are then filled with John Innes Potting Compost No. 3, pushing the compost in all round the basket to make sure it is firm and to get as much compost into the basket as possible. The fuchsias are planted around the top inside edge of the basket; as planting is being done it is advisable to leave a saucer-like depression at the top to make watering easier. If it is not possible to hang the baskets up in the greenhouse then they can be placed in the top of 20 to 23 cm (8 to 9 in.) flower pots and be stood on the greenhouse staging. As the plants become established in the baskets they will require more and more water; at no time must the compost be allowed to get very dry. Gradual hardening off must begin from early May until the baskets are hung outside in late May or early June. From then on they must be watered every day, rain or no rain; not only are the baskets exposed to the warm sunshine and the drying winds, but to the reflective heat from the building as well. On warm sunny days the baskets must be watered at least twice a day, giving sufficient water to soak the compost right through and twice a week at least some liquid fertilizer can be added to the water. Given this treatment, the baskets will continue to make a fine spectacle until late September, or in favourable weather until well into October.

Pests and Diseases

There are but few diseases which affect fuchsias and the only one to be concerned about is *Botrytis* (grey mould). This has a tendency to affect the plants if they are kept too close together during the early part of the year, and there is a tendency to crowd plants together when so many other plants have to be grown in the greenhouse. Good ventilation and a free circulation of air between and round the plants will keep the grey mould down to the absolute minimum. Spraying with a fungicide based on thiram or benomyl will control grey mould.

The most troublesome pests are whitefly, greenfly, red spider mite and mealy bug, but by good management these are not difficult to keep in check. Whitefly can be controlled by spraying with H.C.H. (formerly and recently known as B.H.C.) or malathion. The fumigating and spraying will kill both adult and young insects, but not the eggs which are laid on the underside of the leaves. It is, therefore, necessary to fumigate or spray at intervals of eight to ten days; after three or four such fumigants or sprays the plants should be completely free from whitefly, and the same treatment will keep greenfly in check too. I was taught in my early days of training that 'prevention is better than cure' and this I practise with all my plants to this very day. The problem of red spider mite can be much more serious, the mites being so minute and difficult to see with the naked eye that there is a tendency for severe damage to be done before it is realized what is happening. Whitefly, greenfly and mealy bug tend to cripple and disfigure the young shoots and cause the leaves to be blackened with a mould forming on the honey dew from the insects. Red spider mite sucks the green colouring matter from the leaves which then turn greyish-white and both leaves and flower buds drop off. In a bad attack the plants can be completely defoliated, leaving nothing but web-covered bare stems. Red spider mite is encouraged by a warm dry atmosphere in the greenhouse and hot dry conditions outside. In the early stages of growth, regular spraying overhead with water and keeping a humid atmosphere in the greenhouse will discourage red spider as much as anything else. When the plants begin to flower in the greenhouse and outside, spray with malathion or liquid derris to keep the plants free from red spider.

Mealy bug is more difficult to control; it is the older plants which are more likely to be affected because the insects tend to hide under pieces of loose bark and in the crevices of the older stems. The eggs and the insects themselves are covered with a woolly or mealy substance and this makes it more difficult to get the insecticide to penetrate to the insect and to the eggs. I find a fine forceful spray is essential and again I find malathion effective.

The young shoots of outdoor or hardy fuchsias, and often the half-hardy cultivars planted outside for the summer months, can be crippled by capsid bug. This is a somewhat shy and fast-moving insect and it is not always possible to see them on the young shoots and the branches; a slight vibration, and they fall to the ground. Dusting with an insecticide powder containing

H.C.H. will prevent this damage. In bad attacks the young shoots become completely crippled and the plants will produce few if any flowers.

Cultivars

As I have already said there are hundreds of different sorts of fuchsia and we all have our own particular favourites. I have my favourites and these could perhaps be a guide to anyone growing fuchsias for the first time. I consider one of the most choice cultivars for growing as a pot plant in the greenhouse or conservatory is 'Lord Lonsdale', which has bright orange flowers and an apple-green tip to each sepal. For freedom of flowering there are few better than 'Phyllis', single with rich pink flowers, and in late summer rich reddish purple fruits which make the plant even more attractive; 'Brutus', single, red and purple; and 'Display', single, red and cerise. Among other favourites are 'Marinka', single, all red; 'Mrs Marshall', pinkish white and cerise pink; 'Snowcap', semi-double, red and white; 'Curtain Call', double, pink and purplish red; 'Voltaire', single, red and purple; 'Royal Velvet', double, red and rich purple; 'Jack Shannon', single, all pink; 'Cascade', single, white and deep cerise; 'Blue Waves', double, pale pink and violet blue; 'Flying Cloud', double, all white; 'White Spider', single, all white; 'Mission Bells', single, red and rich purple; 'Fascination', double, red and pink; and 'Swingtime', double, red and white.

The best cultivars for standard plants in my opinion are 'Blue Waves', 'Mission Bells', 'Marinka', 'Mrs Marshall', 'Phyllis', 'Swingtime', 'Voltaire', 'Snowcap' and 'Brutus'; for hanging baskets among the best are: 'Swingtime', 'Mrs Marshall', 'Jack Shannon', 'Marinka', 'Cascade' and 'Curtain Call'.

Hardy Fuchsias

The hardy fuchsias, of which there are numerous cultivars, are among our finest summer-flowering shrubs, beginning as they do in late June and early July and continuing to flower until the frosts of autumn. The secret of growing hardy fuchsias is to plant deeper than would normally be done with other shrubs because the tops in most parts of the country will be killed by frost during the winter months. The stems below ground level however remain alive and give rise to the new shoots the following spring. I prune my hardy fuchsias to ground level in March every year and at that time feed the plants with an organic-based general garden fertilizer and top dress around them with garden compost or peat.

The most vigorous cultivars will grow to 90 cm (3 ft) or more in the one season and continue to flower through until well into the autumn.

Among cultivars I have in my garden and confidently recommend are 'Mrs Popple', red and purple, one of the most vigorous of all; 'Tom Thumb', red and mauve, dwarf and one of the freest-flowering sorts; 'Gracilis Variegata', small flowers in red and purple, attractive variegated foliage; 'Susan Travis', red and pink; 'Alice Hoffman', red and white; 'Corallina', red and purple of somewhat prostrate habit; 'Madam Cornellisson', red and white, free-flowering; and 'Margaret Brown', red and pinkish mauve, vigorous.

Some Favourite Shrubs

S. Miller Gault, M.B.E., F.L.S., V.M.H.

Prunus tenella

W HEN I retired after 50 years in horticulture in various aspects I opted for life in the country in preference to living in a town and was fortunate to settle in a small country cottage. There were some drawbacks. The cottage had been derelict for some years and the tiny garden could not be seen, overgrown trees and weeds had been allowed a free run, undoubtedly to the liking of the bird population but somewhat discouraging to a lover of plants. The restoration of the cottage added to the problems; a wet winter and the consequent high water-table were largely overcome by the builders with bags of cement plus the debris from the cottage. Eventually all was cleared and I was able to take over a small area of the adjacent field in order to accommodate my collection of plants. The neglected field had a wonderful crop of nettles growing so lustily that I was encouraged in the hope that some at least of my plants would copy the example and grow as vigorously. Further encouragement was provided by a healthy *Rhododendron ponticum*, a useful indication that the soil was at least lime-free and ideal for many of my favourite plants. A few soil samples taken at random indicated that the pH was around 6.5, indicating that rhododendrons and heathers, also roses, would be reasonably happy.

With some small trees to provide some shelter, a little privacy and a background, I intended to plant shrubs to ensure that little annual planting would be required, also to ensure that as my energy declined I would be left with some time to contemplate and enjoy my garden. With shrubs as the backbone and the bones, a little flesh would be provided by bulbs and dwarf herbaceous plants.

For many years mixed borders containing shrubs have appealed to me and I have also had a latent desire, brought about by admiration of cottage gardens, to produce such a garden, free from attempts at landscaping or colour combinations, but simply where favourite plants would thrive and look at home. I also attempted to ensure that attractive plants could be seen from the windows as an additional pleasure, especially as many of these plants have been received from friends or by the traditional gardeners' method of exchange.

Some friendships go back a long way, so just inside my gate is a small shrub of southernwood (*Artemisia abrotanum*) whose grey-green finely cut leaves are frequently pinched on entering or leaving, a strongly aromatic reminder of similar bushes in the top county of Scotland where the same plant is likewise strategically placed near the cottage door or gate. It also reminds me of long-departed ladies who brought out a sprig in the kirk as a reviver when the sermons, unduly long, began to pall. Easily grown and easily propagated, this cottage garden favourite, known in more favourable climes as 'old man' and 'lad's love', responds well to hard pruning in spring, a useful attribute particularly in small gardens and one I use to advantage with several of the shrubs I grow, keeping them in scale with my small garden without inhibiting, indeed in some cases increasing, their decorative function.

Gorse, furze or whin (*Ulex europaeus*), according to which part of the British Isles you live, is represented in my garden by the double form 'Plenus', a much superior plant for the garden, being slower and more compact in growth especially if grown on poor or dryish soil in full sun. It is useful also as a hedge, for small boys or marauders of any sort will not readily face its sharp prickles. On warm days particularly, its aroma of coconut brings back memories of extensive displays on Scottish hillsides. I prune my plant hard after its main display is over which lasts for a considerable time in spring.

The Chinese bush cherry (*Prunus glandulosa*) is not all that common in gardens, but is a shrub, especially in its double white form 'Albiplena', of considerable charm. The young growths are rendered pendulous with the weight of the flowers, which are useful if cut early for decoration. If all are cut for this purpose further pruning will not be necessary. A double pink form 'Sinensis' is also attractive and although popular in the past is seldom seen in present-day gardens.

The dwarf Russian almond (*Prunus tenella*) is, like the foregoing, a three-footer which suckers freely and produces a brilliant display of rosy-red flowers in spring unless you have a population of bull-finches. In my garden this year a pair of these beautiful birds acquired a taste for the buds, perhaps increased by the cold weather. I grow the 'Fire Hill' form and prune all flowered growth back to six inches.

The Spanish broom (*Spartium junceum*) can be a tall, leggy, somewhat gaunt shrub if allowed to grow naturally. Pruned in March or April every year, taking care not to cut back into old wood, it becomes a bushy low shrub producing glowing yellow pea-like flowers which have a delicious scent over a long period. These are useful for cutting, lasting quite well in water. It grows best on well-drained soils including chalk, but is less successful on heavy soil.

Rivalling the gorse in many parts of Scotland, bringing golden sunshine to the hills and braes, is the broom (*Cytisus scoparius*), a parent of the many hybrids which are popular in gardens because they grow so quickly and flower so prodigiously. Unless pruned after flowering by reducing the young growths half-way back, they are apt to get leggy and are short-lived plants which require replacement in a few years. I would, however, like to grow 'Lena', a branch sport discovered by Charles Coates on C. 'Burkwoodii' in the Royal Botanic Garden nursery at Kew. Charles passed on in 1978 at the ripe old age of 98 years. His fine plant is very productive of its orange-red and yellow flowers and is of compact habit around 2 ft in height. Ideal for the small garden, I have not so far seen it offered commercially.

Dwarf brooms I grow are the pale yellow C. × *kewensis*, a foot or so high and a yard across, and the more compact C. × *beanii*, a brilliant golden yellow in May, the plant completely smothered when in bloom. I would grow the Warminster Broom C. × *praecox* also because of its fine habit and fine cream and yellow flowers but do not do so; its somewhat rancid odour is too much in my small garden which is all around and in close proximity to the cottage.

The delightful *Genista lydia*, generally around 2 ft in height although twice that in spread, is a favourite shrub of mine and many other gardeners, flowering so freely in May and June that the arching branches are obscured, especially when grown in full sun. Ideal for cascading over a low bank or wall, it can be pruned after flowering, although not really necessary, except in tiny gardens. I also grow *G. pilosa* 'Procumbens', which I find attractive on a well-drained corner. It is quite procumbent and also produces yellow flowers freely over a mat of silvery hairy leaves.

Fuchsias in my garden, as in so many others, are in reality almost herbaceous in character, as the growths which produce flowers so freely in autumn die back and have to be pruned away in April. The most common and hardy *F. magellanica* 'Riccartonii' is too large for me, so I grow 'Mrs Popple', a very hardy cultivar bearing flowers with scarlet sepals and deep purple corolla with great freedom in autumn. With smaller but more graceful flowers *F. magellanica gracilis* adds an air of elegance, and its sport 'Variegata' presents its handsome white-margined leaves with a blush of pink throughout the summer months. The hybrid 'Tom Thumb' at 18 in. is free-flowering and compact, a charmer for a small garden.

The 1978-79 winter has been severe and 26° of frost (Fahrenheit) has been registered in my garden, so I am delighted that *Perovskia atriplicifolia* 'Blue Spire' has come through reasonably well. It gives us tremendous pleasure during July and August, when its beautiful lavender-blue panicles harmonize with the grey-green aromatic leaves. Another plant which I keep restrained by an annual short back and sides with the secateurs is *Senecio* 'Sunshine', known in my early gardening years as *S. greyii*, then more recently as *S. laxifolius*, and now believed to be a hybrid of these two species with possibly another as a bonus. Mixed parentages are not always as pleasing in their result as this fine grey-leaved shrub which when pruned hard, as I invariably do, results in the loss of the clear yellow daisy-like flowers which are the reason for its name. To my mind these spoil the silver effect, which is enhanced by pruning, and indeed is my reason for growing it as it harmonizes its neighbours and readily grows lower growths which touch the soil, frequently root and so are useful as 'give away' plants.

Rigorous pruning is not suitable or necessary for other shrubs I grow such as the Beauty Bush, the popular name of *Kolkwitzia amabilis*, a lovely shrub when smothered with its lovely pink flowers touched with yellow in the throat. My plant is the form raised at the Royal Horticultural Society's garden at Wisley and named 'Pink Cloud', well named indeed, its floriferousness enhanced by removal of a few old flowering growths to make way for young growths to flower next season.

Two willows give me great pleasure. I have often admired the Woolly Willow, *Salix lanata*, which thrives particularly well in the Northern Horticultural Society's Garden at Harlow Car near Harrogate, nowadays in North Yorkshire. I grow the dwarf, somewhat gnarled form 'Stuartii', to my

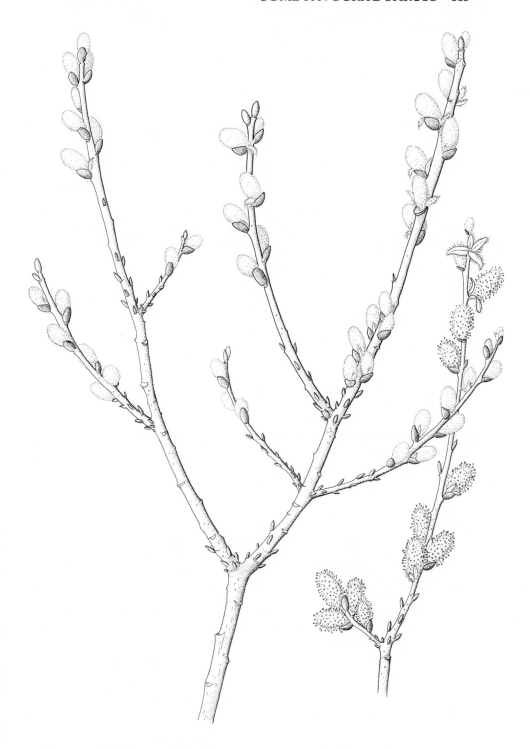

Salix hastata 'Wehrhahnii'

mind an outstanding plant, very effective all the summer by reason of its silvery-grey downy leaves but particularly beautiful in spring when the orange buds spring to life and produce large upright yellow catkins which fade off-grey. Less handsome in summer but superb in spring is *S. hastata* 'Wehrhahnii' with masses of upright silver male catkins which become yellow with pollen in time. A larger shrub than 'Stuartii' which is generally only a couple of feet high, 'Wehrhahnii' is at least double that but more upright in habit. I would like to grow *S. alba* 'Chermesiana' for the winter colour of its orange-scarlet branches when hard pruned, a pleasure I have forgone so far as I would have to harden my heart to make room for it.

I had almost done so and decided to remove *Syringa afghanica* in spite of its delicately beautiful foliage as it seldom produced any flowers. I must have expressed my thoughts aloud as at the time of writing (May) it is handsomely covered with lilac flowers on a shrub 4 ft high, so is reprieved for another season as least.

It is many years since I fell in love with roses and dug up a few suckers of *Rosa spinosissima* growing wild near the cliff tops on the east coast of Caithness. I cajoled them to grow in my boyhood garden and the simplicity of the single five-petalled cream flowers has always appealed to me; indeed I still consider single-flowered roses beautiful especially when, as in *Rosa moyesii* 'Geranium' which I grow, the single crimson flowers are succeeded by large flask-shaped orange-scarlet hips which last in beauty for several weeks. In my garden, this fine Wisley-raised rose attains six feet and is fairly upright in habit, so is very well suited to many gardens except very small ones. 'Scarlet Fire' requires a deal more room, being of arching growth, and demands 6 ft of width at least. The single crimson-scarlet flowers are spectacular in size and colour and in due course are followed by large hips which last well into the winter and are deep red in colour.

The pale yellow *Rosa primula* is pretty in foliage and when in flower, usually in May. However, I usually grow it for the remarkable scent of its foliage, named the incense rose by some because of this feature; it always seems to be at its best on warm, humid summer evenings or after a shower of rain. Not being an authority on incense, the scent always reminds me of honey-filled bee-hives on warm evenings. *R. complicata* grows fairly close to the standard crabapple *Malus* 'Red Sentinel' with the result that the long arching branches of the rose reach up into the lower branches of the tree. Beautiful single flowers are freely produced, very like a much-enhanced dog rose (*R. canina*) in size and colour, being deepish brilliant pink; as is usual with single roses, a crop of hips follow, quite decorative but lacking the brilliance of colour of those already mentioned. One of the smaller *Rugosa* roses which does not require so much space as *R. rugosa* itself is 'Frau Dagmar Hastrup'. It produces the most lovely light pink single flowers imaginable with a crop of large tomato-like hips as a follow-up. Although lower and more compact in growth than other cultivars of *R. rugosa*, it can be pruned to curtail its size further where necessary. Pleasing in habit also is 'Schneezwerg', a *R. rugosa* hybrid which also has the valuable characteristic of recurrent flowering, so much so that the hips from the early flowers intermingle pleasingly with the later flowers. Semi-double and snow-white in colour, these are produced in clusters; consequently the small red fruits also are abundant. At the display garden of the Royal National Rose Society near St Albans this rose has grown into a very fine hedge, aided by a little judicious trimming.

I grow other roses but have no desire to turn this chapter into a catalogue; however, I would not like to leave out 'Golden Wings', again a single-flowered rose with a considerable amount of *R. spinosissima* in its veins. A slightly sentimental attachment arises without doubt, but despite that I grow five plants so that we can enjoy the large single, shapely blooms throughout the summer. I prune hard, not having room to accommodate the 6 ft shrub it can attain if only tip-pruned. The sulphur-yellow flowers are prominently contrasted by mahogany stamens and are continuously produced over a long season and there is a bonus of fragrance, while its parentage ensures its hardihood.

My taste in plants is rather too catholic to be credited with the disease called rhododendronitis, but being on lime-free soil enables me to enjoy a few which have a special appeal. Number one must be *Rhododendron yakushimanum* (abbreviated to 'yak' by those closely associated with the genus and its enormous range). I am fortunate to possess the Exbury F.C.C. form, still unexcelled by the many hybrids which have resulted from its use in breeding. Slow-growing, it will eventually attain a height of 4 ft with a wider spread and is of most distinctive appearance, a rounded mound, with silvery spears of young growth appearing above the dark green leaves. These of course appear after the compact trusses of bell-shaped flowers, deep pink while in bud, a more delicate pink as they open, finally becoming pure white. It is a native of the island of Yakushima, Japan.

R. augustinii is a somewhat variable species as far as colour is concerned and I am fortunately the possessor of a light blue form with a touch of green in its throat. Growing under ideal conditions in a sheltered woodland this species can eventually attain a height of 15 ft. I am glad my plant is only a third of this but flowers freely and having small leaves is most attractive. The Bodnant hybrid 'Elizabeth' is deservedly popular and is surely one of the best for the smaller garden. A spreading shrub around 4 ft, the rich red trumpet-shaped flowers are so freely produced, visitors to my garden are quite enthralled with it. Mine is the First Class Certificate form. My wife was responsible for the introduction of another Bodnant hybrid to our garden, the cultivar 'Seta'. We were visiting the Savill Garden in Windsor Great Park when the somewhat unusual appearance of this pretty hybrid intrigued her with its vivid pink and white narrow flowers.

A few evergreens especially valuable for effect in the winter months are imperative as far as I am concerned, and as I have always had a soft spot for the native Scots pine, *Pinus sylvestris*, I have planted the miniature *P.s.* 'Beuvronensis' which I grew in a pan for a few years, but it is now much more contented in appearance and has attained 3 ft in height and spread. Junipers, now available in a wide range, have long been among my favourite plants, seen on the hills in my schooldays when I used to go hunting for ferns. Years later I saw *Juniperus conferta* growing in the Rock Garden at the Royal Botanic Garden at Kew and was rather surprised to find it sustained little damage during this past very severe winter. Its bright apple-green leaves are most acceptable in winter. When happily situated it can be somewhat rampageous but withstands pruning well and is excellent as ground cover in front of other shrubs. *J. communis* 'Repanda', *J. procumbens* 'Nana' and *J. horizontalis* 'Douglasii' are all prostrate shrubs, decorative and useful for this purpose. To counteract any flatness in appearance I also grow *J. communis* 'Hibernica', the more open Swedish form 'Suecica' and the more recently popular *J. virginiana* 'Skyrocket', the latter standing up better to snow this past winter. I also have a small plant of the hedgehog juniper (*J. chinensis* 'Echiniformis') not often seen in gardens, and a dwarf compact form of *J. communis* found in the island of Harris, which brings me back to Scotland again where my interest in plants was first aroused and followed.

In common with most gardens some climbing shrubs are grown. An old tree stump is rendered decorative by the self-clinging climbing hydrangea (*Hydrangea petiolaris*). A small tree on the boundary acts as host to *Clematis montana* 'Elizabeth', the fragrance from the soft pink flowers of which wafts in through the window of my den as I write. A larger male holly provides a similar service for the more colourful *C. montana rubens*, keeping company with *Lonicera etrusca* which will follow on with its cream and yellow fragrant flowers later in the year.

A Lifetime
among
Rhododendrons

Frank Knight, F.L.S., V.M.H.

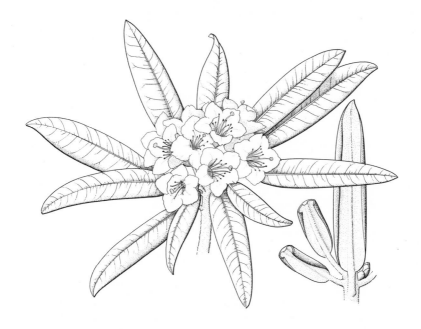

Rhododendron yakushimanum

I SUPPOSE I can justly claim to be an all-round gardener, but more than once in my lifetime in response to the direct question 'Have you a favourite plant?' I have unhesitatingly replied, 'Yes, the rhododendron'.

It all started in my schoolboy days before the First World War when, during school holidays, I would join my father on what is known as the Terrace Garden at Werrington Park, North Cornwall, the property then of Mr J.C. Williams and now of his grandson. My father was carrying out extensive work in the preparation of beds in which to plant rhododendrons raised from George Forrest's seeds which were arriving from western China.

All the background to this work fired my imagination, for I was able to see in the garden the unpacking of the wooden crates of seeds forwarded from Rangoon. (An excellent illustration of a consignment appears opposite page 20 in *The Journeys and Plant Introductions of George Forrest, V.M.H.* published for the Royal Horticultural Society in 1952.)

I have no doubt about the love of plants being uppermost in my mind for the whole of my life. Before I was twelve years old I used to spend many hours, mainly alone, scouring the district around my birthplace for British wild plants and taking specimens to school where a special table was set aside on which there were glass jars containing water to receive them. I used the local common names and when we were 'stuck' for identification we waited for a visit from the school attendance officer, who was an expert on British plants. This interest in the British flora has never diminished. At the request of the Director, Sir Arthur Hill, I parted with the collection of herbarium specimens which I made during my student-gardener days at Kew, so that this could be forwarded to a herbarium at Carlesburg, New Zealand.

But to return to rhododendrons. The day came when I was asked if I would like to work in the gardens at Werrington Park. This I gladly accepted and because war had broken out and all the young men on the estate had 'joined up', I found myself as a garden-boy doing responsible work which under normal conditions would not have come my way for three or four years. There were fourteen gardeners with a very well-planned staff layout and promotion came from the beginning through the role of journeyman and so on. But this was never re-established after the war.

George Forrest was my hero; he was in western China collecting new plants and we were at the receiving end in the propagating houses doing our utmost to raise young plants from his seeds. Very careful records were kept and I soon learned the importance of the collector's field notes and numbers. I cannot describe the excitement of seeing plants flower for the first time in cultivation. We had to be patient and wait for the rhododendrons, but there was also a great collection of Chinese *Primula* species. I could write much about these and the care that was taken to provide them with growing conditions in accordance with Forrest's field notes. *Primula forrestii* was spectacular in the stone walls while *P. nutans* under the canopy of *Magnolia wilsonii* trained into small single-stemmed trees had to be seen to be believed.

I have written an account of some of the rhododendrons at Werrington Park in the *R.H.S. Rhododendron and Camellia Year Book 1966*. I return to Werrington Park as often as I can, but sadly I am now the only one left who saw the beginnings of forming the unique collection there.

Time marches on; the war ended and the survivors of the garden staff who had enlisted returned, a few with war wounds which handicapped them. Economics demanded that numbers must be reduced from pre-war days and those of us who had been last engaged were asked to seek other employment. A new Head Gardener in the person of R.M. Gregory from Mr J.C. Williams's other estate at Caerhays Castle had been appointed. R.F. Fitt, who had been the Head Gardener, had left to take charge of Endsleigh; he is commemorated by *Rhododendron fittianum*.

Dick Gregory, as the new gardener was affectionately known, was newly out of the Forces and he was sent to the Royal Botanic Garden, Edinburgh for a refresher course among George Forrest's plants being grown there. He came to Werrington Park full of praise about the training provided for young probationer-gardeners there. This fascinated me and we approached 'Mr J.C.' and asked if he thought I would stand a chance of being accepted for the three-year course. He was dubious about an Englishman being eligible, but 'we would see'. The result was that I was offered one of the places available, and off I went in December 1919.

The three years spent in the Royal Botanic Garden, Edinburgh would make a story in its own right. To begin with I was baited and fought the Battle of Bannockburn over and over again. I was not the only Sassenach, for one of my colleagues was Harold Comber from Nymans, who subsequently undertook plant-collecting expeditions in the Andes and Tasmania.

The life of a probationer in those days was very arduous and discipline was very strict: there were long hours of practical work commencing at 6 a.m. in the garden and lectures and examinations in the evenings. But for me, I was in the very heart of rhododendron introduction and cultivation. Professor (later Sir) Isaac Bayley Balfour was our chief and life was exciting.

I saw the original planting of the wonderful collection of *Rhododendron* species in the large glass house especially built for them. I had the good fortune to work for nearly two years directly under that greatest of all plant propagators – Laurance Baxter Stewart. He had the gift of imparting knowledge, often by no means gently. George Forrest lectured in the large lecture theatre between hours during my time in the garden.

The next 6½ years were spent in the Arboretum at the Royal Botanic Gardens, Kew, first as a student gardener, but the position of Arboretum Propagator, which had been in abeyance since William Purdom left Kew to go plant-collecting in China in 1909, was restored by the Curator, Mr W.J. Bean, and I was asked to fill this. These were among the happiest years of my life. There was the great freedom of caring for the Arboretum nurseries, the adaptation of the existing propagating pit and frames to comply with what I had been trained to do at Edinburgh, the great wealth of plant material in the gardens and the continuous arrival of seeds from all over the world. These included rhododendrons from Forrest, Kingdon-Ward and Joseph Rock; those from Forrest via Mr J.C. Williams.

During one of his visits to the gardens, 'Mr J.C.' – as I continued to know him – was brought to the Arboretum nursery by Mr Bean to see me. He simply said 'Well, don't think you know anything until you have passed 60'. This really pricked my balloon; I was young, red-haired and thought at that time I knew it all, but in retrospect how right he was. 'Mr J.C.' must have remembered his visit, for it was followed by a gift of 'Forrest's Field Notes' beautifully bound and inscribed 'From Mr J.C. Williams, Sept. 27th, 1926 and sent from his Scottish estate, Strathvaich, Ross-shire'. A neighbouring book on my bookshelves is a copy of *Farrer's Last Journey* by E.H.M. Cox, inscribed in his handwriting 'F.P. Knight from Euan Cox, Dec. 1926'.

My work at Kew involved propagating rhododendrons from cuttings; this was rather a new subject at that time but I had good results especially from any rhododendron derived from *R. caucasicum*, an early parent, with *R. arboreum* and others, of some of the best early hybrid cultivars.

Another incident among many of those days was that in the absence from Kew on the same day of W.J. Bean and Arthur Osborn I was deputed to take Mr E.H. Wilding of Wexham Place, Stoke Poges around the Arboretum, and within two days of his visit he sent me an autographed copy of his book *Rhododendrons, Their Names and Addresses*. Some years later, following the death of R.M. Gregory at Werrington Park the copy of this book presented to him by J.C. Williams was given to me and my original gift from the author is now in the Wisley Library.

On another day I was gathering cuttings from some of the rare plants growing around King William's Temple when George Forrest appeared, all alone. We chatted for quite a while and he asked me if I would like to go with him on his next expedition to western China, but nothing came of this. I believe I am one of two people similarly invited, the other being Robert Lindsay of Windsor Great Park, previously at the R.B.G. Edinburgh.

The mention of taking cuttings reminds me I was once successful in raising a single plant of *Rhododendron afghanicum* from the only specimen growing at that time in the Rock Garden.

Although life was undoubtedly pleasant there were no prospects of promotion in sight, so I took a very bold step and entered the nursery trade by joining the very well-known firm of Bakers of Codsall. Here I had two main charges, the Alpine Plant Department and the landscape planting of the many gardens made by the firm; this included the complete overhaul of Selfridge's roof garden.

Rather remote from rhododendrons, but one Sunday in the spring of 1930 in company with James Baker (at that time Chairman of Wolverhampton Wanderers) and his younger brother Norman and Charles Nunn, the head of

Rhododendron catawbiense

the Tree and Shrub Department, I made my first visit to Bodnant. We were entertained by Mr and Mrs F.C. Puddle, one of the most memorable days in my life.

Then back to rhododendrons in a big way. In 1930 the firm of Anthony Waterer established at Knaphill in 1796 was being reconstituted under the managing directorship of F. Gomer Waterer. I was engaged as first nursery manager and then general manager. This gave me a great opportunity to bring into operation my knowledge and experience of raising rhododendrons, this time in commercial quantities. This work I enjoyed for ten years; there was a team of first-class craftsmen, I had the freedom to up-date the propagating equipment and the backing of a wonderful collection of hardy hybrid rhododendrons and of course the world-famous strain of Knaphill azaleas. It was exciting to discover there a number of American azalea species and what was said to be a specimen of *Rhododendron catawbiense* from the original introduction from North Carolina, U.S.A. by John Fraser in 1809.

I spent much time carefully hybridizing among the Knaphill azaleas, and many now in cultivation with names of birds originated from this work. I also crossed many evergreen rhododendrons and of these I particularly like 'Sapphire' and 'Nimbus'.

Exhibiting rhododendrons at R.H.S. shows formed an important part of the firm's programme. I remember the first group of choice plants I staged as a table exhibit. This contained a lovely specimen in flower of *Rhododendron taggianum*. It was while in charge of this group I first met Capt. (now Major) A.E. Hardy, who grows rhododendrons so well at Sandling Park in Kent.

Gomer Waterer was a past master at timing rhododendrons to flower for specific shows; there was a minimum of wasted plant material. I learned a lot from him, based on the breeding of the plants being got ready; he knew instinctively from their origins whether they needed gently pushing along in warmth or gently retarding by placing them in cooler conditions. Mr E.H. Johnstone of Trewithen recorded in his report of the annual rhododendron show in 1931: 'On the stand of Messrs Gomer Waterer – surely never did plants look so fat and well grown, there was not a leaf that complained of the treatment it had received'. In 1938 the Knaphill exhibit gained the Rothschild Cup.

Alas, when we were really settling down and beginning to enjoy the fruits of careful work in reclaiming the nursery, the Second World War broke out. I shall always remember walking up that long straight road in the centre of the nursery with Gomer Waterer when, quite spontaneously, he said 'Well, Knight, it was a long, long time to look forward to, but now it seems such a short time to look back on'. We had become good friends.

I left Knaphill, became Senior Horticultural Officer in the Directorate of Camouflage, Ministry of Home Security, and did not return to the nursery. I was told that labels of the crosses I made had become lost and many of the plants resulting from controlled hybridizing had to be sold as mixed unnamed seedlings. I often wonder what happened to them, for some must have been good plants.

My wartime job came to an end in March 1944 and for the next ten years I managed Notcutt's nursery at Woodbridge, where the soil was alkaline and rhododendrons were not produced. I have nevertheless kept in touch with my favourite plants and appreciated being invited to serve on the R.H.S. Rhododendron and Camellia Committee and to act regularly as a judge at shows, including that at Truro. I kept my interest active by contributing articles on rhododendrons, particularly their propagation, and visited as many rhododendron collections as I could including those in Scotland and N. Ireland.

In 1955 I was appointed Director of Wisley Garden and this meant close contact with the great collection of rhododendrons there. A valuable hybridization programme had been and was being carried out by Francis Hanger and among plants he raised are 'Beefeater', 'Billy Budd', 'Burma Road', 'Lady Bowes Lyon' and the 'Moonshine' group. There too were the major trials of hardy hybrids. I attended whenever possible the special Committee which judged these and delivered a comprehensive lecture about them at the International Rhododendron Conference of the American Rhododendron Society in Portland, Oregon in 1961. Later in North Carolina I contributed two

Rhododendron arboreum

talks, one on 'The breeding of yellow-flowered hybrids in the U.K.' and the other on the work done so far in raising hybrids from *Rhododendron yakushimanum*.

In 1968 I was invited to give the Banks Lecture in Wellington, New Zealand, and my tour extended so that I could spend some time in the beautiful setting of the Pukeiti Rhododendron Garden near New Plymouth. I took with me slides of noteworthy rhododendrons at home.

An experience which proved very exacting was that of being appointed by the R.H.S. Council to act as Steward at the annual rhododendron show for all the classes of hybrids. I feel I brought to this work some useful knowledge on classification, but I know too that with each succeeding show I learned a great deal. I always regarded the Monday before the opening day and the early hours of this as two of the most demanding days of my year's work. I rarely reached home on the Monday evening before 11.30 p.m. and I was away again from Wisley by 7 a.m. next day.

Every now and then, Mr H.H. Dividson who came from R.B.G. at Edinburgh to deal with the classes for species would reject an entry saying 'this is a hybrid, it belongs to you'. I never had the good fortune to find a species among my hybrid entries so that I could send it to him.

Talking of exhibiting I recall the lovely groups which were staged from Wisley at Ghent and Hamburg. I was elected Chairman of the special committee which compiled the list of 'Hybrid Rhododendrons usually available' which was printed in the *Rhododendron Handbook 1969*, part 2.

Since retirement at the end of 1969 much enjoyment has come my way from my continuing to be connected with rhododendrons. In the revised version of Vol. III of *Trees and Shrubs Hardy in the British Isles* by W.J. Bean. I contributed the section on rhododendron propagation.

Great pleasure came from the guidance which Helen my wife – who had typed for Professor Bayley Balfour – and I provided for Mr and Mrs J.D. Johnston of North Carolina in finding the right rhododendron specimens to photograph among the best of the collections in the U.K. We travelled extensively, working long hours to get the pictures, and we were made so welcome and given so much help by the owners of many well-known gardens. This work is described in *The Garden* for July 1977 and resulted in a gift of over 600 coloured slides of rhododendrons to the R.H.S.

In return we spent many pleasurable days with the Johnstons in their lovely home in Baltimore Forest in North Carolina and botanizing among the wild rhododendrons. To this I should add our trips to the West Coast where we were the guests of the Brydons at Salem, Oregon, the McKinnons in Eugene and Dr Philts on the Mackenzie River where *Rhododendron austrinum* impressed me so much.

I have been indeed fortunate in being able to spend more than 60 years doing what I most wanted to do, and value more than I can say the award to me in 1975 of the Loder Rhododendron Cup.

Trees for a Small Garden

J.R. Hare, M.V.O., N.D.H.

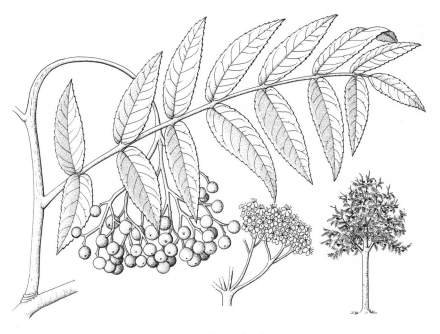

Mountain ash

T HE URGE to grow at least one tree at some time or another overtakes most people. The countless thousands of acorns, peach and avocado stones and apple pips which are planted each year in flower pots or yoghurt containers and stood on window sills bear witness to this. And very commendable too, but there are numerous small-garden owners who heartily wish they had resisted the urge. A familiar sight in suburban streets in front of a neat semi-detached is a pair of funereal cypress trees flanking the gateway or the front door and dwarfing everything else. These were purchased and planted, in good faith as dwarf conifers, nice little upright evergreen trees in miniature. But they weren't really dwarf conifers at all and they grew and grew until eventually they stand, gloomy brooding monsters, completely dominating the garden and the house. Another common sight is the weeping willow, planted alongside a little ornamental pool in a back garden. It looked so nice in its early years with its fringe of yellow twigs waving in the breeze and its lovely pale green leaves, the first to unfold in early spring. Then, after a few years it began to take over. Its lovely branches spread until eventually the whole garden and even part of the house is in shade. The little pool is full of dead leaves and the hungry roots spread even farther, robbing the other plants in the garden of their share of water and nourishment. And yet the various forms of *Chamaecyparis lawsoniana* – Lawson cypress – the usual offenders, and the weeping willows, *Salix babylonica* and *Salix* × *chrysocoma*, are, in the right place where there is room for them to develop, handsome trees.

The would-be tree owner should make sure before he plants that there will be room for the tree of his choice to grow to its full size without disturbing the balance of the garden, without affecting the growth of other plants and without unduly shading the windows of the house. The right sort of tree in all but the very smallest of gardens can be a tremendous asset. It gives a feeling of permanence and an air of maturity which nothing else can give. It can provide interest over long periods and at different seasons, even in the winter, and above all perhaps there is the satisfaction, which I know means a lot to many people, of owning a tree.

The most popular small trees are those which flower in the spring, particularly the cherries, and there are hundreds of them to choose from. However if there is room for only one tree, is a glorious splash of colour for a few days in the spring enough? This is all that can be expected from many of the cherries which, after one wonderful week, can look rather dull for the rest of the year. There are cherries which have more to offer and these are among my favourite small trees.

Anything which flowers in winter is worth considering and *Prunus sub-Hirtella* 'Autumnalis', the winter – or autumn – cherry, does just that. It produces its small semi-double white or pinkish white flowers from November on throughout the winter, in mild spells often finishing with a burst of flower in March. Another cherry to brighten the winter garden, but in a different way, is *P. serrula*. It grows quite quickly to about 20 ft and its glory is its shining reddish brown bark which glows like polished mahogany in the winter sunshine. It has small white flowers in the spring, but as these open with the foliage they are relatively insignificant.

The foliage of some of the cherries colours well in the autumn, and one of the best is *P. sargentii*. This tree grows to a somewhat larger size than the previous two, reaching about 30 ft, with a neat rounded head. Quite early in the autumn, this is one of the earliest trees to show autumn colour; the leaves turn through golden yellow to orange and red.

Despite my earlier comments, there are two small cherries which don't do very much but flower in the early spring but which do it so well that I am including them in my short list. One is *P.* 'Accolade', a hybrid between *P. sargentii* and *P. subhirtella*, a wonderful sight in March–April with its masses of clusters of semi-double pink flowers, and the other is *P. incisa*, often seen as a large shrub, which has pink buds opening to white, usually in March. The small leaves frequently colour nicely in the autumn.

Because my subject specifically concerns small gardens I must not miss out *P.* 'Amanogawa' (also called *P. serrulata erecta*), which grows slender and erect like a small Lombardy poplar. It has large pale pink flowers but, despite its obvious advantages in confined spaces, it was never a favourite of mine, often appearing rather gaunt or spindly.

The flowering crabs vie with the cherries in their wide variety and profusion of bloom in the spring, usually later than the cherries. Many of them also have conspicuous and, in some cases, edible, fruit. I suppose the fruit of all cultivars must be edible, but only a few are palatable when eaten straight from the tree. As they generally have denser crowns than the cherries, the crabs cast more shade and consequently they are less easy to fit in with other plants, but some of them must rank as among our finest flowering trees.

Important among the crab apples is the Purpurea group, with purple-tinted foliage and fruits. *Malus* × 'Lemoinei' is one of the best with its large crimson-purple flowers and strongly purple-tinged foliage. Another one with similar colouring but with slightly smaller flowers produced a little later is *M.* × 'Profusion'. Others similar in colouring and habit, and both splendid trees, are *M.* × 'Eleyi' and *M.* × 'Purpurea' itself. All these are particularly useful, quite apart from their displays in flower and fruit, because their purple foliage contrasts so well with the predominantly green foliage of other trees and, of course, grass.

My favourite crab is *M. floribunda*. This does not have tinted foliage or anything special like that. It just smothers itself every spring with masses of bright red buds which open to palest pink or white. In flower this little tree is really beautiful.

Lovely though they are, the crabs and cherries are perhaps rather commonplace. They are very popular and they grow almost anywhere, so long as they can get their heads in the sun, and they are easy to plant and care for.

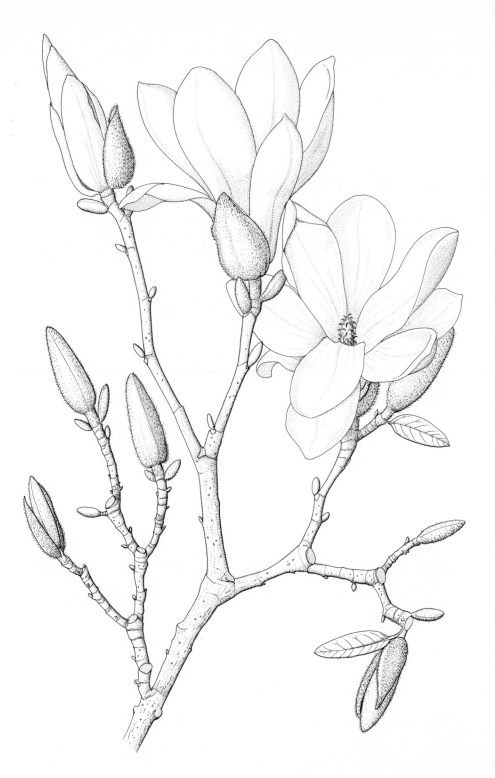

Magnolia x soulangiana

They are reasonably priced and readily available and they quickly grow large enough to make a reasonable show.

Rather more difficult and requiring a bit more patience are what I think are the aristocrats of the spring flowering trees, the magnolias. The easiest and probably the most rewarding of these, because they flower early in life, are M. × soulangiana and M. stellata. M. × soulangiana is the larger of the two and it opens its large goblet-shaped purple-based white flowers in April before the foliage appears. If it can be sited where its flowers are seen against a (hopefully) blue sky, the effect is quite magnificent. Once established and if it likes its situation, it will grow fairly quickly and, unlike some of the magnolias, it will produce its first flowers when only 3 or 4 ft high. M. stellata is slower-growing and usually earlier-flowering. Its flowers are pure white with numerous narrow strap-like petals opening to a starry shape, hence the name. If one accepts the definition of a tree as a plant with a single stem (a trunk) and a shrub as a plant which branches out from ground level, or just above, then these are both really shrubs, M. × soulangiana reaching about 15 ft high and as far across, more in a good situation, and M. stellata being rather smaller. Magnolias require careful handling in their early years. I prefer to plant in spring, when the roots can grow away quickly and, as it is very important that they should not get too dry in their first year, it is a good idea to use peat or leaf mould generously, worked in the soil round the roots and as a mulch. M. × soulangiana will tolerate lime in the soil, but a neutral to slightly acid soil is preferred, and is necessary for some other species. As my chosen magnolias open their flowers early in the year it is obvious that these are likely to be damaged by frost or cold north or east winds, and if they can be provided with some shelter from these quarters it will be to their advantage.

The lilacs are really large shrubs, though occasionally one sees them, looking rather stiff and awkward, growing on 5-ft stems. There are many garden kinds of the common lilac (Syringa vulgaris) and they are all good value. They are easy to grow in most soils and conditions, except heavy shade, and they are tolerant of moderate urban pollution. Many of the cultivars available are of French origin and some are double-flowered. I prefer the singles and I think the traditional lilac scent is important but, unfortunately, some of the garden sorts are less fragrant than the common lilac. If I had to choose just a few of the available cultivars I would go for 'Vestale', which is pure white and quite beautiful; 'Firmament', an attractive pale blue; and 'Souvenir de Louis Spaeth', a rich wine red. All these are good garden plants and, most important, they all smell of lilac.

One of my favourite trees is the native mountain ash, the rowan of Scotland, Sorbus aucuparia. It is not an ash at all but a member of the rose family, like the crabs and cherries, and it is quite suitable for small gardens as its growth is slender and open. It is attractive in flower, its neat ash-like foliage is pleasing and it is the first of the berry-bearing trees to produce its brilliant clusters of ripe red fruit in the late summer. For this reason, because it is a harbinger of autumn, marking the close of another summer, it does remind us that the years are ticking away, but it is a lovely tree and I can forgive its impatience.

The mountain ash has a well-known cultivar bearing the name of *S.a.* 'Beissneri' which is an upright-growing tree, stiffer in habit than the rowan, and its chief attraction is its orange-brown bark which seems to intensify its colour when the leaves fall. This is a tree to brighten up any garden in the winter.

The ubiquitous sycamore volunteers its unwanted seedlings everywhere and it can be a nuisance to the soft-hearted gardener who cannot bear to pull these up once they develop beyond the seed leaf stage, but it does have some interesting relatives. The snake bark maples are fascinating and unusual small trees. Their dark green bark is marked with irregular strips of white, or white and pale green, to give a most attractive marbled effect which shows up particularly when the leaves have fallen. The foliage of this group of trees colours well in the autumn as a bonus, and altogether these neat handsome trees are an asset in any garden. There are several species which display this snake bark characteristic, in particular *Acer grosseri*, *A. pensylvanicum*, *A. davidii* and *A. hersii*. Another maple with distinctive and very attractive bark is *A. griseum*, the paper bark maple, so called because the old bark on the trunk and main branches peels off in papery flakes to show the satiny pale orange-brown new bark below. This is one of the best maples for autumn colour.

In August or September a sight to remember is *Eucryphia × nymansensis* covered with its large creamy white flowers set against glossy dark green foliage. This handsome evergreen is not the easiest of plants to grow but when it finds its feet in the right place it is perhaps the finest of all summer-flowering trees. It will grow to about 15 ft but its width is usually no more than half that. It is not quite hardy in the north except in very sheltered places, and in fact it always pays to plant this tree out of reach of the full blast of north and east winds. Slightly hardier but still to be treated with care is *E. glutinosa* which is deciduous or only partially evergreen and which bears masses of white flowers in July and August.

Hardy anywhere and, I think, our most beautiful native tree is the silver birch, *Betula pendula*. I never think it is at its best as a solitary specimen but if planted in a small group of three or five, on a grassy mound in a corner of a garden – and I appreciate I am not now dealing with what most of us would consider to be a really small garden – a feature which will be a joy for many years will have been created. If the grassy mound can be liberally planted with daffodils, preferably one of the early flowering cyclamineus hybrids, 'February Gold' or 'Peeping Tom', and bluebells, the result will be delightful. The silver birch, in nature a woodland tree, is very accommodating. It even does well, quite out of its environment, as a street tree, but I think it looks out of place in any sort of formal arrangement. The graceful beauty of its slender drooping twigs, always moving in the wind, and its small leaves shimmering in the sun is something few other trees can match. With its graceful outline and its silvery grey bark the silver birch really earns its title, the lady of the woods.

There is one silver birch which can be grown in quite small gardens and which does not look out of place planted alone as a specimen tree on a lawn, or by a pool. This is Young's weeping birch, *B.p.* 'Youngii', a much better weeping tree in a confined space than the weeping willows.

So far I have mentioned only one true evergreen and, although these have to be sited with great care when room is limited because they can cast heavy shade where it is not wanted, in the house as well as in the garden, there is a special charm about plants which hold their foliage and give colour, even if it is only dark green, in the winter. Some of the many cultivars of holly, particularly those with silver or gold variegation, are suitable for small gardens providing the owner does not object to their annoying habit of dropping their leaves in late spring. Personally, although I admit that hollies are very useful as park trees to give variety of form and colour I find it hard to get enthusiastic about them as garden trees.

An evergreen which is much more suitable for a moderate-sized garden is a close relative of the common hedging privet which, incidentally, when it is not clipped and chopped about, is not without attraction as a large background shrub. I refer to *Ligustrum lucidum*, which is a handsome bushy tree with narrow pointed lustrous leaves and panicles of white flowers, not unlike lilac, in the autumn.

An evergreen tree, or large shrub, with a lot of character is *Arbutus unedo*, the strawberry tree. This member of the heather family, a native of the Mediterranean region and southwest Ireland, is hardy in the south and west, and unlike most of its relatives it will tolerate some lime in the soil. It has white or pinkish flowers in drooping panicles during the late summer and autumn, ripening its large strawberry-like fruits of the previous year at the same time. The fruits look delicious but, although they are edible, they are disappointingly insipid. In favoured areas, when the fruits ripen in large numbers, the effect is quite striking.

I began this chapter by sounding a warning about planting so-called dwarf conifers which cause embarrassment by developing into comparatively large trees. There is an attraction about conifers which many people find irresistible and, in closing, I would mention a few which can be safely planted in confined spaces. There are plenty of really dwarf conifers available which sprawl along the ground or form tightly packed cones or domes no more than 2 or 3 ft high, but as these can hardly be classed as trees they cannot be discussed here. I am restricting my choice to a few which can be expected eventually to reach from 5 to 12 ft. *Chamaecyparis lawsoniana* 'Minima Aurea' is a lovely little tree, very slowly growing to 5 ft, with tight-packed golden yellow foliage which is very much appreciated during the winter. Another very useful cypress is *C. pisifera* 'Boulevard', which forms a broad-based cone about 10 ft high. Its feathery foliage of silvery blue overlying green is quite distinct and it is in plentiful supply in most garden centres.

For people who like their conifers to stand like sentinels flanking a gateway or door there are two junipers which fit the bill admirably, or they can be used with dramatic effect singly or in small groups among dwarf shrubs or heathers, for instance. *Juniperus* 'Sky Rocket' will eventually form a flexible column up to 15 ft without spreading much more than 15 in. A truly remarkable tree. *J. communis* 'Hibernica', the Irish juniper, slowly grows to about 12 ft or more in a less narrow but more rigidly columnar form with tightly packed branchlets. For those who really have pocket-handkerchief gardens and who hanker after pencil-slim conifers there is *J.c.* 'Compressa', the best of the truly dwarf columnar conifers, which rarely exceeds 3 ft. Unfortunately this is not usually a long-lived plant and it is less hardy than most. For the larger garden and when longevity is desired, the upright-growing Irish yew and its golden variant are fine trees. *Taxus baccata* 'Fastigiata' will take many years to reach 15 ft, having eventually a 3 or 4 ft spread. With its typical dark green yew foliage this is a rather sombre tree and it needs careful placing. The golden form *T.b.* 'Fastigiata Aureomarginata' is a more amenable garden plant. As they grow older and broader these trees are liable to damage by heavy snow and they need to be carefully tied in with pliable wire.

Finally, another well-known and deservedly popular golden conifer, probably the best of all for colour, is *Thuya occidentalis* 'Rheingold'. This tree tends to be somewhat variable in form but it is usually a broad-based cone up to 10 or 12 ft. With its strong winter colouring of coppery gold it associates very well among winter flowering heathers and contrasts well with the varied greens of other conifers.

Fruit Growing
in a
Small Garden

Horace Parsons, A.H.R.H.S., N.D.H.

THE MODERN trend in housing estates leaves very little scope for the enthusiastic gardener; even the so-called executive-type house often has the bare minimum-sized plot with no option for the owner to purchase more land to enable a fruit garden to be developed. If it is possible to make good borders at the base of the walls of the house without damage to the footings, these do offer excellent opportunities for trained tree fruit-growing. My own house is 50 years old, and ten years ago I made new borders with fresh soil at the base of all the walls where it was practical to do so. On the west side, one fan-trained sweet cherry 'Early Rivers' and two 'Morello' cherries; I would have liked more sweet cherries but they take up a lot of wall space and as there are no easily available dwarfing rootstocks for them, lifting, root pruning and replanting in alternate years in their youth may become necessary to curb excessive growth and induce fruitfulness. 'Morello' cherries, however, present no such problem, seldom, if ever, failing to crop prodigiously. The fig, propagated from February-inserted cuttings in a warm greenhouse and therefore on its own roots, often grows too luxuriantly to crop satisfactorily and confining its roots in a container such as a brick cubicle $2 \times 2 \times 2$ ft ($60 \times 60 \times 60$ cm) on a concrete bottom with a suitable drainage hole is ideal. 'Brown Turkey', 'Brunswick' and 'White Marseilles' are those most frequently grown, but a friend gave me a little tree which I think is the cultivar 'Castle Kennedy'; it crops very well indeed in a confined border against my garage wall facing east, and is fan-trained. Nearby with the same aspect I have two grape vines: one is the white-berried dessert 'Buckland Sweetwater', the other is the red-berried wine grape 'Siebel 13053', which is also quite pleasant to eat when quite ripe and thrives surprisingly well against this east wall. A fan-trained peach 'Bellgarde' occupies part of a south wall of the house, and although the fruit quality leaves nothing to be desired it is small-flowered and, at blossom time, I often wish I had planted the large, pink-flowered 'Peregrine' or 'Amsden June'. In planting peach trees out of doors, one should always remember that glandless-leaved cultivars are very susceptible to mildew; 'Royal George' (small-flowered), 'Dymond' and 'Early York' (large-flowered), for this reason, are best avoided for planting out of doors, excellent though these all are for growing under glass. Out of doors, peaches, like nectarines, are very subject to the crippling fungus disease peach leaf curl; it is controlled by spraying with either 3% lime-sulphur or a liquid copper fungicide in mid-February. I usually repeat this spraying during the first week in March, but keep to one form of spray in the same season. The almond tree is also sprayed with this fungicide at the same time.

The west wall of my house is somewhat shaded by a neighbour's high wall but even so, I have devoted this to seven cultivars of upright cordon pears 8 ft (2.4 m) in height, budded on to quince rootstock 'A'. The border was made up of good loam 18 in. (45 cm) deep and 3 ft (90 cm) wide and is kept well watered during the summer, as otherwise it would become too dry for pears. In choosing cultivars, some that I would have liked were unobtainable and some

I knew to be a little unreliable here in Norfolk. It is pointless planting cultivars, however excellent their fruit, if they seldom crop. The following therefore were planted: 'William's Bon Chrétien' ('Bartlett' in U.S.A.), 'Louise Bonne of Jersey', 'Emile D' Heyst', 'Conference', 'Beurré Superfin', 'Doyenné Du Comice' and 'Glou Morceau'. The first six are too well known to need comment; in three years out of four, 'Glou Morceau' is an excellent late pear but about every fourth year its fruit is very disappointing and only fit for cooking. This collection ripens more or less in succession from September to Christmas, in sufficient quantity for my household's dessert. We would like more 'William's', which is about the finest pear for cooking and bottling. Stewing pears, in my opinion, are not worth growing in the garden. 'Catillac' is the most frequently grown and possibly the best and I am often asked how best to cook it. Each fruit should be peeled, cored and quartered, put in a casserole with some sugar, a little water and cloves or lemon peel to flavour, then placed in a slow oven and allowed to cook for two hours or more until tender.

Grapes

I have one electrically heated and automatically ventilated greenhouse $12\frac{1}{2}$ ft (3.8 m) long in which I have planted two grape vines, one at each end. This is really too ambitious, as such a greenhouse can barely accommodate one and I will have to discard one eventually. At the south end is 'Muscat Cannon Hall', one of the best white grapes which, to do it justice, requires more heat than I can afford to give it, but which nevertheless, even in the unfavourable season of 1978, produced some quite presentable bunches. It is, however, a cultivar that I would not recommend to the novice grape grower, as it can be very disappointing unless properly treated. In common with white grapes generally, the berries require exposure to the maximum available light, even to the point of tying up the overhanging leaves away from the bunches, in order that the berries develop that amber colour which is consistent with the highest quality in white muscat grapes. Black grapes, on the other hand, must have a good canopy of foliage over them to exclude light from the berries, otherwise they fail to end up the jet black which is the hallmark of a well-finished bunch. At the north end of the greenhouse is a young black muscat 'Mrs. Pince'. This is a most excellent grape with a muscat flavour which I think will tolerate the moderate heat that I maintain. It has large bunches of medium-sized berries which are thick-skinned and hang in good condition longer than some other cultivars including 'Black Hamburgh'. The latter is more often grown and is probably the best black grape for the unheated greenhouse and a good partner for white-berried 'Buckland Sweetwater'. For exhibition, 'Gros Colmar' has very large black berries in quite impressive bunches which will ripen quite well most years in an unheated greenhouse, though a better finish for exhibition is obtainable with a modicum of artificial heat. The flavour of the berries in either case, however, is inferior to that of

'Black Hamburgh' or 'Esperione'. 'Foster's Seedling' is another good grape for an unheated greenhouse, its large white berries almost equal to those of 'Black Hamburgh' for flavour, but their thicker skins enable the bunches to be kept longer. Few persons, other than experienced grape growers, appreciate the extensive root ramifications of which the grape vine is capable. When growing a vine in small greenhouses it is highly desirable to thoroughly prepare a fairly extensive border exclusively for them outside. It is common practice to plant grape vines outside the greenhouse and run the main stem or rod through a hole in the side or end of the greenhouse. However, I prefer, whenever possible, to prepare equally a section of border inside the greenhouse adjacent to the outside border, tunnelling beneath the greenhouse footings to connect the two. The vine planted inside the greenhouse will quickly send roots under the footings into the outside border. After three or more years, few roots will be found in the inside border but the outside one, if it was properly made and not dug over for vegetable- or flower-growing, will soon be a mass of roots, the surface of which should be dressed annually in January with a proprietary vine fertilizer or, failing this, dried blood, bonemeal and John Innes Base Fertilizer, then mulched with stable manure.

Training of the top growth is quite simple; the main rod is kept upright to 12 in. (30 cm) below the glass roof, then turned beneath the roof midway between eaves and ridge towards the far end and stopped at a convenient point. Wires run lengthwise of the house; to these the fruiting laterals are tied in, right and left, each stopped at two leaves beyond the first formed flower-bunch of buds, one bunch only on each lateral. Sub-laterals are stopped by pinching after one leaf, unless more leaves are required as a canopy over black grapes.

After setting, reduce the number of bunches to the required crop and thin the berries at the size of sweet pea seeds; first tie out the shoulders so that they hang clear of the main bunch. These shoulders require much less thinning than the main bunch: commence at the bottom of the latter, leaving one berry at the tip, remove all seedless berries, thinning the remainder so that a lead pencil can be moved freely amongst the berries, using a pair of grape scissors and a short forked twig to manipulate the bunch, as the berries are ruined by handling or touching with the hand. The vines are kept mainly to the western side of the greenhouse, where the glass reaches to within a foot of the ground. It is half-glass on the east side, with a bench covered with gravel trays from the heated propagator to the south end, where cucumbers, melons, tomatoes, vegetables, and ornamental seedlings are raised for growing elsewhere.

Apples
Restricted forms such as cordons, espaliers and dwarf pyramids on dwarfing stocks offer by far the most practical means of growing a continuous

succession of dessert and culinary cultivars of apples from July or August until April in the small garden. One learns from one's mistakes but it is much less painful, and often less expensive, to learn from other people's. A common mistake is to plant a vigorous 'Bramley Seedling' in a small garden. To illustrate this point I quote the particulars of one such instance: a tree of bush form on a short trunk 2 ft (60 cm) high measuring 5 ft 2 in. (1.5 m) in circumference at 18 in. (45 cm) above ground, with a branch spread of 28 × 30 ft (11.4 × 9 m) and over 20 ft (6 m) high. Although difficult to estimate the extent of the shading of this tree, its roots occupy 136 square yards. The tree is too large to spray with the owner's knapsack sprayer. It crops well most years, but much of the fruit is blemished or falls early, being attacked by sawfly larvae. In contrast to this, ten years ago I erected a 6 ft (1.8 m) high angle-iron and galvanized wire fence and planted against it 45 'Malling No. 26.' rootstocks 2 ft 6 in. (75 cm) apart. In the following July they were budded with a selection of 27 cultivars of dessert and culinary apples, training the resultant maidens as oblique cordons. The latter cast very little shade as the row runs north-south; the roots occupy 115 square yards of land. A spraying programme is comfortably carried out with a pneumatic knapsack sprayer and last year's crop was between 12 and 13 bushels, covering the home-grown apple season until well into April. There are nearly 2,000 apple cultivars in the National Collection at Brogdale and it would be pointless listing those which I grow. In addition, I am an apple enthusiast and change cultivars from time to time by grafting or rebudding with scions or buds kindly given me by interested friends.

Plums

There are no definite dwarfing rootstocks for plums as there are for apples and pears, and unless one resorts to root-pruning and close pinching of the summer growths the trees are very liable to become too large for the small garden. The fan-trained spur-pruned form against a wall or fence appears to be the most accommodating for the small garden, but training as pyramids is also possible. Experimentally, I tried the method which was not uncommon in large private gardens before the war, when some of the choicest gage plums were grown in 12 in. (30 cm) clay pots or in tubs, in unheated greenhouses. These are closely spurred in compact pyramidal form, the summer soft-growth pinching being similar to that carried out with apricots. Using the cast-iron ribs from two dilapidated Nissen huts as a framework, a lofty 9 ft (2.7 m) high curved-roof fruit-cage was erected and covered with ¾ in. (2 cm) netting. In this were planted a collection of plums ten years ago, each restricted to 8 ft (2.4 m) in height and to 4 to 5 ft (1.2 to 1.5 m) at their widest point; lifting and root-pruning in their early years checked their tendency towards luxuriant growth. They have proved to be a great success. Dessert cultivars planted were 'Kirke's Blue', 'Jefferson', 'Count Althann's Gage', 'Bryanston' and 'Coe's Golden Drop', while 'Early Rivers', 'Ouillin's Gage' and 'Warwickshire Drooper' provided culinary fruit.

Damsons 'Shropshire Prune' and 'Farleigh' outgrew their allotted space in my garden; I grubbed these and retained only a half-standard damson 'Merryweather' which, sprayed occasionally from December until April with bird repellent against bullfinches, crops well most years.

Soft fruit

Between the plums are bushes of blackcurrant 'Laxton's Giant'. The large sweet berries are much more even in size than those of 'Boskoop Giant'; they are hard-pruned immediately after gathering the fruit.

Also in this cage are two short rows of raspberry 'Malling Jewel', some cordon redcurrants 'Red Lake', and several sorts of cordon gooseberries. For some years I grew raspberry 'Phyllis King', a fine cultivar, often shown by the raiser, who took several first prizes at the R.H.S. July Shows with it, but my stock became infected with the mosaic virus and had to be destroyed.

The indispensable raspberry 'September' is grown in the open without netting, as birds rarely, if ever, take the fruit; these berries, freshly gathered in September and October, and quite often in August, are much preferred to summer raspberries preserved in the deep freezer. All canes of this are cut right down in February, as the fruit is borne on the tips of the current canes.

Although there are plenty of wild blackberries in the vicinity, the 'Oregon Thornless' blackberry is greatly favoured, as it does not have the objectionable large seeds of some of the other cultivars. It has a flavour very near that of the wild blackberry and, as it is unarmed, the berries are more comfortably gathered.

Lack of space forced me to reduce my loganberries, youngberries and Japanese wineberries to two plants each, but I retained a row of boysenberries, of whose large juicy berries we are very fond when served with cream and sugar. Indeed, we regard it as the best of the hybrid berries. The Japanese wineberry is an attractive novelty with its bristly red stems and yellow and red sweet fruit, again very nice served with cream and sugar. Like the raspberry and blackberry, these fruits are pruned after the fruit has been gathered by cutting the old canes to the ground and tying the current canes in their places. Owing to the limited ground space in the fruit-cage, the hybrid berries are trained from ground to roof strings; any lateral growths are shortened after the third leaf and the canes tipped at 8 ft (2.4 m).

Even in quite a tiny garden, strawberry growing is possible; the Continental cultivars such as 'Gento' or 'Triplex' with their larger berries are quite good, but I have confined my strawberries to 'Cambridge Favourite', a commercially grown sort which I find more convenient for covering with large barn cloches. To amuse the young children of visitors, I sometimes grow a patch of alpine strawberry 'Baron Solemacher', raising it from seed sown in the warm greenhouse in February, the plants being set outside in May and fruiting in August.

The site for a few bushes of blueberries was originally excavated and filled with acid peat and a little well-rotted manure, but they have never fully recovered from the two dry summers of 1975 and 1976 when watering restrictions were imposed. With the blueberries, pruning consists of thinning the bushes by cutting out the oldest growth to near ground level during dormancy.

Other fruit

After planting quince 'Meech's Prolific', I was presented with the Yugoslavian cultivar 'Vranja', which has much larger fruit. This is less suitable for the small garden, being a stronger grower. They were trained as half-standards. It soon became apparent that we were overdone with quinces, so the 'Meech's' was dug up and given to a friend.

It is with tongue in cheek that I mention my last tree fruit – *Malus* 'John Downie'. The fruit of this lovely ornamental crab is quite the best I know for making crab-apple jelly, and in half-standard form, the tree is an acquisition for both fruit and floral display.

Melons

The fastest-growing of all our fruits, melons can be grown in the smallest garden providing they get abundant sunshine, this being essential for the best quality in these most luscious of fruits. In the warm greenhouse or in frames over a hot bed, the casaba melon cultivars can be grown to perfection, individual fruits weighing anything from 3 or 4 lb (1.35 to 1.8 kg) up to 12 lb (5.4 kg). 'Sutton's Universal', 'Ringleader', 'Superlative', 'Emerald Gem' and 'Hero of Lockinge', also 'King George', are all excellent if one can obtain seeds of them. In the cold frame and beneath cloches it is the cantaloupe melons such as 'Ogen' and 'Sweetheart' which have become the most popular. These are small-fruited and I aim at six fruits per plant. Seeds are sown singly in small pots of sandy soil in a warm greenhouse timed to plant into cold frames or under large barn cloches at the end of May or early June, when their second rough leaf is about the size of a 10p piece, stopped at the fourth or fifth leaf to develop four leaders in a frame or two under cloches, when the laterals carry the requisite number of female flowers (the latter have an embryo fruitlet at the back of their petals). A fully open male flower is selected for each pollination, the petals removed and the remains of the flower inserted into the female on the third day. Successful fertilization will be indicated by the swelling of the fruitlet, when feeding and top dressing should commence.

Vegetables for Chelsea

H.J. Dodson, A.H.R.H.S.

P RODUCING vegetables for Chelsea Show needs a good many items –
such as greenhouses, cold frames and cloches and some good shed
space. A supply of experience gathered over the years by growing a wide
range of crops to a deadline is also important. The latter provides knowledge
of cultivars which will give good results under the many changing conditions
one must expect between December and May. There must of course be
adequate time for all the detailed attention required for the production of
show vegetables for any show. For Chelsea Show however, one needs not
only time but an excess of dedication and skill that springs from a great love of
the job. One must of course love one's wife above all else, but to produce 26
kinds of vegetables in 72 cultivars for Chelsea Show calls for a love of the job
second only to one's wife. Of course if you are fortunate enough as I to have a
wife who also loves the work, well, it then becomes a very blissful pursuit. I
must also mention that as Head Gardener to the gardens of a country estate I
also needed and was blessed with an employer who also loves his garden and
in due course is happy to underwrite the bills.

It takes several months of hard work preparing potting soil for the many
items needing pot and box culture in the early stages. Hot beds have to be
made in the frames, often in the bad weather of January and February, plus
seed beds to be made up on these hot beds. Other frames must also be made
ready for plants when moved out of the greenhouses. These are pleasant
enough jobs when the weather is set fair, but when it turns so suddenly
against you as our late winter, early spring weather can, that is when the love
of the job has to push you to the limit. Carrots, beetroot, spinach, potatoes,
turnips and kohl rabi all need to be sown at this doubtful time of the year.

However, there are some pleasant winter tasks which can be carried out in
warmth and comfort, notably ordering seeds, manures, insecticides,
fungicides. In addition, a good sound list of all the items intended to exhibit
must be drawn up, including everything required for their cultivation.
Growth of these crops under glass is often so rapid that anything likely to be
required for their well-being must be on hand.

Those lovely little carrots so enjoyed in May must be sown in frames and
cloches just after Christmas and certainly by 19 January. This is at a period
when most people are still enjoying Christmas and New Year activities. In the
bad winter of 1962-3 we actually removed snow from a border which had been
prepared for our cloche carrots. A little added dry soil and sand made a tilth;
the seeds were sown and clipped up all in a day. Carrots were pulled from
this sowing for Chelsea.

Every week brings fresh jobs to add to the burden of the long-term crops
growing under heated glass. Then comes the difficult spell when frame and
cloche crops need attention and the weather really says stay indoors. Warm
clothing must be put on and out you must go to thin carrots, beetroot, spinach
and turnips. Of course, those items in the heated greenhouses do not stand
still while you are out of doors; they need feeding, tying and spraying and

constant watch on the temperature and ventilators. Sudden bursts of sunshine during March and April soon cause soft spindly growth, and somehow the most difficult and trying weather always comes at weekends when no staff are around and you probably have friends staying. It is such spells which test your skill and love of the job. On top of all this one usually has quite a lot of other garden to keep up. I had also many acres to maintain and to keep a supply of fresh vegetables, flowers and fruit for the house.

Our last exhibit of vegetables at Chelsea was produced without the aid of any artificial heat and yet it contained twenty different sorts and 70 cultivars. The first item sown was leeks fourteen months before the Show, spring cabbage ten months, cauliflower eight months, while January and February saw the bulk of the crops sown under the cloches and frames. Potatoes were grown in pots and frames; turnips sown early March under cloches and frames. The latter are delicious in May, as of course are the carrots, whether one exhibits or not. Radish were always grown under cloches, taking approximately five weeks to reach maturity. Always the last item to sow was the mustard-and-cress, four or five days before the Show, which always meant the growing of it had to finish while we were at the Show staging the exhibit. The latter task required $2\frac{1}{2}$ days, not to mention a day beforehand at

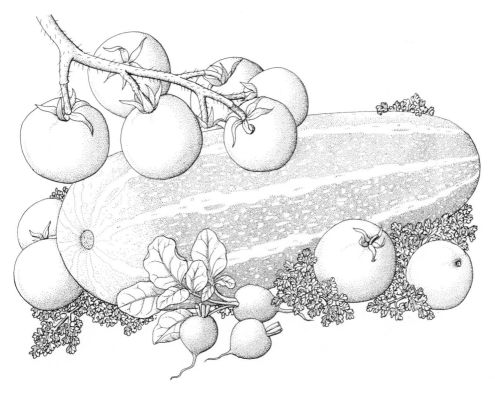

the garden putting such items as leek, lettuce, beet, carrot, turnip and rhubarb into their baskets and packing them safely so that they would travel without harm. Vast quantities of parsley were used to pack around them in the lorry and to push in between all the root vegetables before they were placed on the staging.

Some of the greatest excitement always came during the gathering of the produce. It is a lovely sight to see these early vegetables being lifted, then washed, quickly dried, selected and packed away in tissue and labelled up, all receiving the care of delicate china. This work was always done at a more comfortable place in the sheds, very often sitting on boxes or stools and talking of past shows, remembering last time's mistakes and knowing not to make them again. The list of items collected and packed would be checked and re-checked and so would every other item, over and over again. Thursday and Friday before the Show were very busy, and one finished dog-tired but usually very satisfied also. Loading the lorry was always hard work and the same again when one arrived at the Show, often having quite long distances to carry the hampers.

Then came two days of really loving the job and placing each vegetable in its basket and showing it off to the best advantage. Even so, one also wondered if it would all be done in time, if one had enough material, would it become too warm and spoil the lettuce and other soft items. Cauliflowers quickly lose their colour in heat, the mustard-and-cress flops disastrously over the boxes and parsley goes yellow overnight, spoiling the fresh look of the whole exhibit. On one occasion we well remember, the wind was so rough a section of the tent split above our heads; the noise and the flapping was really frightening. My employer's wife came to see us staging but quickly left us, and the cold on this dreadful Sunday evening was something one does not expect in May. However, after much hard work the time comes for the staff to go and you are left with that glorious hour or so when the judging takes place and you get your note that you may be presented to the Queen or a member of her party (I was presented to the Queen Mother, Prince Philip, Princess Alexandra and the Duchess of Gloucester, in different years during our four Chelsea Exhibitions). Next comes the great joy when one sees the much sought-after Gold Medal Card placed on one's exhibit and one feels great pride and satisfaction, especially when the crowds come in and throng around your exhibit. Every day brings fresh faces and old friends and old memories are relived. All the difficulties somehow fade away and somewhere inside you a clock starts ticking over, making plans for next year before this exhibition is even cleared.

And what a game clearance of one's exhibit is. People start to collect around you long before the final bell sounds, waiting to purchase your produce; what a scramble it turns out to be, everyone needs the same dish at the same time. One fears for the old and tries to serve them first and in a very short space of time one is forced up on to the staging for safety. What has taken months of

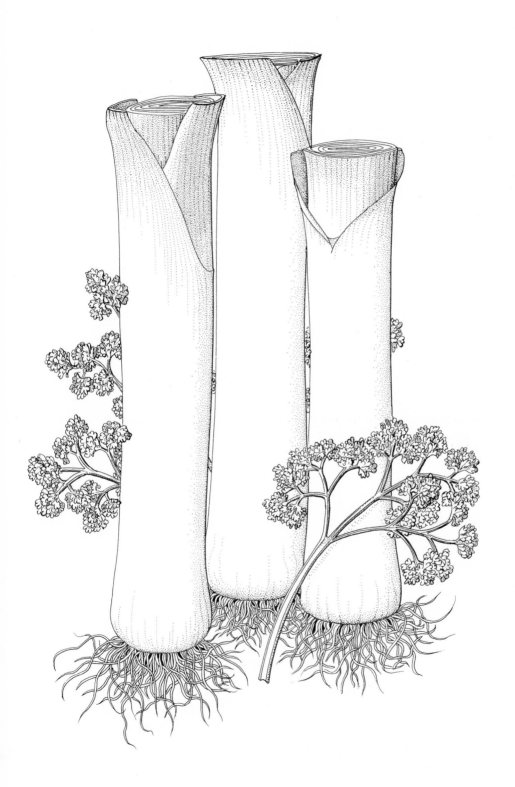

hard work, love and care to produce, prepare and stage is dismantled within an hour and the staging looks a dreadful mess of empty baskets, spilt parsley and moss; this has to be cleared up and left clean and tidy as you found it. Then your own gear has to be packed up and loaded – what fun and frustration that can be – lorries are let in according to regulations, very little space to spare can be found, often the lorries have to keep moving and hampers thrown on the moving vehicles. Somehow we get loaded and on the road for home, arriving back any time between 11 p.m. and 1 a.m. Then unloading has to take place because the hired lorry must be returned. What a sad job it always seems to be clearing out the baskets and packing boxes and storing them away for another year. Only one happy task remains, that of hanging up the Gold Medal Card in the Garden Office and thanking those who helped and those who wrote kind notes of congratulations.

Growing vegetables for show is a hard game few will wish to attempt. The techniques required, however, can provide much-appreciated early crops for the home kitchen. Indeed, every small garden should have a frame and a few cloches devoted to vegetables. Early carrots can be sown during January and February, lettuces planted under cloches in March will be ready for cutting at Easter. Turnips sown under cloches and a few potatoes in a cold frame in early March will mature in late May. October-sown cauliflowers over-wintered in a cold frame and planted out in late March will give excellent heads in early June. Peas sown under cloches in early February with lettuce planted on either side are very worthwhile. Radish can be sown under cloches from late February at two-weekly intervals. Beetroot sown late February-early March begins to mature late May. Dwarf beans can be greatly advanced by sowing under cloches or in a frame in early April.

The Joy of
Water Gardening

Philip Swindells

Waterlilies

F OR ME a pool is the loveliest and most rewarding feature of a garden: the quiet gliding of goldfish amongst verdant lily pads and chaste blossoms – the soft tinkling of water from cascade or fountain, and the gentle swaying and rustling of rushes in the breeze – fresh and exciting experiences which one can only compare to the first glimpse of aconites through winter snow, the rich earthy aroma of well-made leaf-mould, or the sweet warbling of the song thrush heralding the arrival of spring. A pool opens new and unexpected vistas to the gardener and provides him with a window on another world, a watery world where new pleasures and mysteries abound.

Yet before one can successfully introduce such a feature to the garden it is essential to lay bare at least some of these mysteries, or else one may reluctantly have to agree with that great gardener William Robinson, who wrote in his *English Flower Garden* 'Unclean and ugly pools deface our gardens . . . the filth that gathers in stagnant water and its evil smell on many a lawn'.

Beneath the water there is a delicately balanced environment in which plants, fish, and snails depend upon one another for their continued existence. Plants provide life-giving oxygen for fish and snails, while they reciprocate by depositing waste material which is rich in mineral salts. Fish also consume insect pests, and snails assist considerably in the control of unsightly and troublesome algae. However, this does not all happen by accident and the correct ratio of plants and livestock must be introduced at the outset if the venture is to achieve any measure of success.

One cannot be dogmatic about the quantity of plants that should be introduced, but when dealing with functional plants it is essential that they be used liberally, although not excessively. Submerged plants carpet the floor of the pool and compete with water-discolouring algae for available mineral salts, while floating subjects assist by casting untenable shade on the water beneath. Marginal plants are purely decorative, and so for the most part are ornamental fish. But these also make a valuable contribution to the well-being of the pool and live and breed happily when introduced in small numbers.

A pool is therefore a totally different proposition from any other the gardener may contemplate, and as a self-confessed 'aquaholic' I must impress this upon the reader. How sad I feel when I see a gardener who is skilled in all other aspects of his craft, stumbling amongst the minefield of pitfalls which pool management becomes in the hands of the uninitiated. However, a basic knowledge combined with the sense that is inherent in all good gardeners invariably brings satisfactory results.

Once bitten by the water gardening bug, even the most ardent chrysanthemum fancier or alpine enthusiast temporarily forsakes his love. For water gardening has a fascination of its own which is shared by young and old alike.

I well remember first becoming interested in the properties of water as a small boy when I had to walk the mile or so to school down a rough farm lane. During winter the pot-holes in the track would be filled with water and at this time it was a delight for us boys to wade through these puddles and 'break up the sky'. Reflections of clouds or trees were destroyed with a well-aimed boot and the resulting concentric rings of ripples were an added bonus. I often call this to mind when I look in my own pool at the long drawn-out shadows of trees and the reflection of puffy white clouds scudding across a bright blue sky. My inclinations are not now to destroy the scene, but rather savour it and marvel at the perfection of the mirror-like image before me.

The use of water in this way can have a quite startling effect upon a garden, giving unexpected illusions of space and grandeur, particularly if used in an informal manner with its surface uncluttered by plants. But water has many other moods. The gentle murmur as it passes over a rocky bed, the crashing fury of a mountain stream, and the thin swaying shower of droplets created by a fountain and transformed into a shimmering cavalcade of colour by the summer sun – all can be used to advantage in the garden.

Water naturally congregates at the lowest point on a landscape and this should be re-created in the garden. A pool that is constructed in defiance of nature looks artificial, and is only acceptable in a formal setting where it is raised above the ground with a brick surround. Its proximity to other features must also be considered, for both aquatic plants and ornamental fish demand an open sunny situation. Overhanging trees and buildings that are likely to cast shade over the pool for much of the day should be avoided.

Trees normally associated with water gardening must also be treated with caution. Weeping willows have leaves that contain a substance harmful to fish, and the pendulous cherries are, rather unsportingly, the winter hosts of waterlily aphis. In fact I do not favour weeping trees for poolside planting at all. Only when used on a grand scale beside river or lake do they have anything to offer. The image by W.H. Davies – 'A lonely pool, and let a tree, Sigh with her bosom over me' – finds no place in the practical garden. Sadly, shade and falling leaves are not conducive to a healthy, balanced pool.

Installing a garden pool is most exciting, particularly when it is one's first venture. However, excitement must not be allowed to cloud judgement and haste is no substitute for patience, for unlike a new flower bed it is not easily moved or modified. Time spent securing the correct position and outline is as valuable as that taken to decide the construction and planting. I find it difficult to imagine what the finished scheme will look like. Even a plan that is drawn to scale has little meaning. So I take a rope or a length of hosepipe and make an outline to the finished shape of the pool. If the pool is other than pre-formed, then this can also be used to mark out the area for excavation.

Having been involved with water gardening for many years now, I have probably used all the techniques of pool construction available: the primitive puddled clay method which was once widely advocated, traditional concrete, pre-formed plastic and fibreglass, as well as rubber, polythene and PVC liners. All, except the puddled clay, have their virtues and are suited to different situations. Pool liners are the most versatile as they will mould to any fanciful shape the gardener cares to contrive. They are particularly valuable for formal pools with sheer sides which in a concrete construction would require complicated shuttering. Pre-formed pools are attractive and durable, but are available only in sizes and shapes offered by the manufacturer. Often these have fussy niches and contortions, inadequate accommodation for marginal subjects, and are produced in unnatural greens and blues. However, should one discover a suitable shape in a more sombre grey or stone, then it should be acquired, for of all the materials available for construction, fibreglass and plastic are the most durable.

A pool alone can hardly be called a water garden. Nature seldom leaves a pool without a supporting cast: a swampy area leading into the water and thronged with all manner of floral delights; sometimes a cascade tumbling and bouncing over rocks and splashing tiny crevice plants in its wake, or maybe a lazy winding stream ambling through – all make a considerable contribution to the pool and can be used effectively in a water garden. In addition man has contrived the fountain, a splendid innovation whereby moving water can be seen at its best.

Due consideration must be given to the inhabitants of the pool though. It is of little use trying to establish waterlilies in turbulent water or beneath the constant spray of a fountain, for they are lovers of peace and tranquillity, natural inhabitants of still pools and quiet backwaters. Most other plants are reasonably tolerant, although a number are happier in placid waters. So are goldfish and their decorative cousins, but golden orfe love to leap in the spray of a fountain or swim against the current of a stream.

Planting a pool is extremely pleasurable, for the hard work is over and artistry begins. Functional plants must of course be incorporated, but these do not detract from the finished picture, a glistening canvas that awaits framing with rushes and painting delicately with waterlilies, not in a wild abstract way, but a tasteful blending of water, plants and surroundings that is pleasing and restful to the eye. So many pools are over-planted. Two or three well-chosen groups of marginal plants and a solitary resplendent waterlily have a much better effect than a dozen assorted kinds clustering at the poolside in a vain attempt to create continuity of colour and interest.

Of course the first thing to consider when choosing suitable plants is the role they are intended to play. Those with a job of work to do must receive immediate consideration, especially the submerged varieties. These are the plants we affectionately call weeds and are usually of a rather sombre appearance, at least the most popular and prolific commercial kinds are. But there are a number of decorative species which are certainly worth seeking out and incorporating with the more traditional sorts.

The lovely water violet, *Hottonia palustris*, with handsome light green whorled foliage and spikes of delicate lilac blossoms held well above the water, is a late spring- or early summer-flowering aquatic and an admirable companion for the water crowfoot, *Ranunculus aquatilis*. Once a common native, this has sadly gone into decline, a decline which we should arrest by making more use of it in our ponds. It is a plant of great beauty with finely divided submerged foliage, dark green lobed floating leaves and exquisite blooms of white and gold. Curled pondweed, *Potamogeton crispus*, is another native, but is not particularly noted for its blossoms. These are tiny, crimson and white, and just emerge above the water. Rather it is the foliage that is beyond compare: serrated and undulating translucent leaves of bronze or rich purplish-green clustered together on succulent stems.

Submerged plants are generally most accommodating and require a little in the way of a growing medium as they are capable of absorbing mineral salts directly from the water. Indeed, some kinds like the hornwort, *Ceratophyllum demersum*, spend half their life rooted and the remainder free-floating. But compost of some kind is generally necessary as most need to put down roots to anchor themselves. Plants from the nursery are usually disconcerting, for they appear as bunches of cuttings fastened together with strips of lead. Although seeming to be clinging precariously to life, once introduced to the water and planted in a container they quickly initiate roots and grow away strongly. The lead weight should be left in position when planting takes place, but carefully buried, for if it remains exposed it rots through the stems and the entire bunch of cuttings disintegrates.

With the machinery of balance installed below, the visual effect of subsequent planting can be considered. Surface shade is a subsidiary to submerged plant growth in maintaining a healthy environment and is particularly important in small areas of water. Large ponds and lakes depend upon it much less and here artistic talents can have full rein. Unfortunately most of us are restricted by circumstances to a pool of modest proportions, but with a little care beauty and business can be combined.

Ranunculus aquatilis   *Butomus umbellatus*   *Caltha palustris*

Waterlilies are the principal providers of surface shade and in many cases the sole reason for a gardener building a pool. And what gorgeous plants they are. The eleventh-century Chinese writer Chou Tun-I describes the waterlily perfectly – 'How modestly it reposes on the clear pool, an emblem of purity and truth. Symmetrically perfect, its subtle perfume is wafted far and wide; while there it rests in spotless state, something to be regarded reverently from a distance, and not to be profaned by familiar approach.'

Of course waterlilies are not always white as is commonly supposed. 'Escarboucle' is crimson, 'Sunrise' yellow, 'Amabilis' pink and 'Graziella' rich copper; 'Esmeralda' has blossoms streaked with pink and white, while 'Aurora' passes from yellow through orange to red. Some have plain green leaves, others mottled, while 'Arc en Ciel' is splashed with rose and white. Indeed, the diversity of colour and form amongst the hardy waterlilies is quite astonishing and in addition embraces varieties that will grow in as little as 15 cm (6 in.) of water as well as those that prefer in excess of 90 cm (3 ft).

Not all colour need be provided by waterlilies, for there are marginal subjects and deep-water aquatics which can be used to considerable advantage. I would not be without the heady vanilla fragrance provided by the striking black and white blossoms of the water hawthorn, *Aponogeton distachyus*. Nor would I want to miss the spring display of marsh marigolds, especially that lovely double form of our native kingcup, *Caltha palustris*, with its waxy golden buttons, for these provide colour long before the waterlilies have stirred. Aquatic irises too are particularly welcome, their bold upright foliage and brightly coloured blooms standing to attention and providing a guard of honour for the impending waterlily display.

I do not favour bright colours at the poolside later in the season, as this is a time to enjoy waterlilies without distractions. A foil of reeds or rushes is very welcome, but not coarse natives which will choke the pool in a couple of seasons. Well-behaved characters like the zebra rush, *Scirpus tabernaemontani* 'Zebrinus', are what are needed. Or 'Bowles' Golden' sedge, the corkscrew rush *Juncus effusus* 'Spiralis', and that tiniest of reed maces, *Typha minima*. The sagittarias or arrowheads have interesting foliage and so does the pickerel weed, *Pontederia cordata*. This has soft blue flowers quite late in the season, and together with the delicate pink *Butomus* can be recommended as attractive without being obtrusive.

Ornamental fish bring movement to a pool: lazy goldfish basking in the sun, fantails and moors wriggling about in the shallows and energetic orfe leaping for flies. An occasional glimpse may be caught of a dusky tench as he gropes around for elusive gnat larvae, or one may witness the regal parade of a Nishiki Koi carp and his concubines.

The water garden provides an ever-changing landscape where nature is in harmony and man can be at peace. Another world, where we can escape the pressures of modern living and for a short time enter wonderland – just like Alice.

House Plants Old and New

Richard Gorer

Chlorophytum

M ANY YEARS ago when I was young and hopeful we never used the
adjective Victorian without a sneer. Anything Victorian was quite
obviously in the worst of taste and very old-fashioned. Few gardeners nowadays can use the adjective without a slight feeling of envy. There seems to
have been no aspect of gardening which the Victorians had not tried and, to
my surprise, they went in for house plants in quite a big way. In the 1880s
Robinson's paper *The Garden* printed a series of articles from Regel, the
director of the Botanic Garden at St Petersburg, in which he listed the plants
that he considered best for keeping in the house, and most of the plants that
we grow nowadays can be found in his list. It does not seem to have occurred
to him that bromeliads were suitable for growing indoors, but he did recommend the elks-horn fern, *Platycerium bifurcatum*, which I certainly thought
was a recent discovery.

The Victorians had to cope with two disadvantages that most of us nowadays can avoid. The main disadvantage was that the atmosphere in towns
was considerably more polluted then than it is nowadays. There were no
Clean Air Acts and, since coal was the principal fuel both for domestic heating
and for commercial establishments, while gas was the principal instrument
for illumination, the air was full of impurities from soot to sulphur. The other
problem was the irregularity of the heat in winter. Houses were usually
heated by coal fires in open grates, which would be allowed to go out at night
and were relit some time during the following day. Rooms tended to get very
hot during the early part of the evening, but later the temperature would drop
alarmingly, so that house plants that would tolerate these hostile conditions
were essential. Among the plants most used were the Indiarubber plant, the
silk oak *Grevillea robusta*, the hardy *Trachycarpus fortunei* (a fan palm), and the
variegated *Aspidistra*, which was then known as the parlour palm and the blue
gum. Variegated ivies were also popular. To cope with the polluted
atmosphere the plants were often grown in glass cases, which could be quite
large. It was often recommended to build an extension indoors from the
window, so that a minature greenhouse resulted in which a selection of plants
could be grown. Nowadays we tend to call such things terrariums, but the
principle is the same. Shirley Hibberd, that great Victorian gardener, called
them a *hortus fenestralis* and there were two kinds. One was portable, so that it
could be removed during the summer to allow more ventilation. This was
always on the inside of the window. The other projected outside the house
and Hibberd averred 'It is an elegance peculiarly adapted for the window that
commands an unpleasant look-out, or where inquisitive eyes impose a limit
on privacy, or perhaps tongues that defy propriety make unseemly noises
without'. In other words it was just the thing to discourage nosy neighbours.
These exterior window gardens were more or less confined to hardy plants
such as small evergreens during the winter, while flowering plants could be
added during spring and summer. The interior one was more ambitious and
Hibberd's example had it surrounded by a wire arch up which German ivy,

Senecio mikanioides, was trained, while underneath were such plants as caladiums, dracaenas, coleus and selaginellas, with a Norfolk Island palm in the centre. It reads oddly to have caladiums and coleus for winter decoration and they could certainly have been replaced by more suitable subjects.

The Victorians liked ferns much more than we appear to do nowadays and since ferns usually are shade-lovers, a fern case was a particularly suitable object for the interior of rooms. Some were quite sizeable. Hibberd mentions one that was 4 ft long and 2 ft high and wide. Normally the cases were situated near the window, but during hard frosts they would be moved into the centre of the room. It was therefore recommended to mount the cases on 'well-built frames with powerful brass castors', so that they could easily be moved. Originally ferns were grown in hermetically sealed Wardian cases, but later it was felt that it would prove beneficial to allow occasional ventilation. Under the case was a tray of water and under this tray a small oil lamp to keep the water warm and thereby heat the case. There seems no reason why this contrivance should be reserved for ferns; any plant with ornamental leaves would surely thrive under the same conditions. However in the latter half of the nineteenth century the number of ornamental ferns available was very large and they had the advantage of looking attractive for the whole year.

It might be interesting to consider the main list of ornamental-leaved house plants that were recommended in the 1880s. There were a large number of agaves, which nowadays we eschew because of the spines on the ends of the leaves. On the other hand aloes are still grown. Our old friend the *Chlorophytum* was then called *Anthericum*. Five plants then known as *Aralia* must now be sought for under *Dizygotheca*, *Panax* and *Oreopanax*. They had four araucarias (nowadays we have only one, *A. excelsa*, the Norfolk Island Pine). Plants rarely seen nowadays are the variegated giant reed *Arundo donax* and a variegated bamboo, *Arundinaria variegata (fortunei)*. Who now has seen *Nolina recurvata*, then known as *Beaucarnea*? That and the related *Dasylirion acrotrichum* are like rather fine-leaved agaves and might well be worth reintroducing as house plants. Eventually they get quite large, but might well be ornamental when young plants. Cordylines and dracaenas might be expected. It is rather amusing to see that the *Cordyline* known as 'Tricolor', which arrived a few years ago as an exciting new introduction, turns out to be *Cordyline terminalis* 'Guilfoylei', which was a novelty in the early 1870s, not the 1970s. Besides the Indiarubber tree two other *Ficus* were recommended: *F. chauvieri*, with leaves larger than *F. elastica* and now regarded as a form of the banyan, and *F. porteana*, which according to the R.H.S. *Dictionary* has leaves 2 ft long and a foot across, which sounds somewhat spectacular and might well be reintroduced. Besides *Grevillea robusta*, two other members of this genus were recommended, though neither of their names seems to be current to-day. Lomatias are rarely grown as house plants nowadays, although they do have elegant foliage. The form of *Osmanthus heterophyllus* with gold-margined leaves is nowadays very rare, but being to all intents and purposes

Dieffenbachia picta

Dracaena deremensis 'Warneckii'

Zebrina pendula

Peperomia caperata

hardy it should be a good house plant. Roupalas are proteaceous trees from South America which are never seen nowadays outside botanic gardens, yet three different species were recommended in the last century. In addition to all these there were 21 different palms from which to choose, including one with variegated leaves. Of course palms and ferns were great favourites in the last century, and their virtual disappearance for indoor decoration is a little hard to explain.

The main trouble with growing plants in dwelling houses lies in the small amount of light that is available, even in a well-lit situation. It does appear, however, that after a time plants become adapted. When they were first tried as house plants African violets were extremely difficult to keep in good condition. The leaves were liable to produce unsightly blotches if any cold water fell on them, or even if the plant was watered with too cold a liquid. Nowadays this does not seem to happen. We are still told to have the water at the temperature around 60°F or 15°C and it is certainly advisable to do so, but it does not seem to be disastrous if this is not done. Indeed African violets are now much tougher plants. Last year I moved into a new house and found I had inherited a couple of these. They had not been watered for some time and looked thoroughly unhappy, but quite rapidly came back to a reasonable condition when properly treated. They are not among my favourite plants and tend to be somewhat neglected, yet they are flowering regularly about every two to three months. The original *Saintpaulia* would have died far earlier.

One of the odd omissions in the Victorian house plant list was *Begonia rex* – odd because the plants were extensively grown and even used for sub-tropical bedding outdoors during the summer. The explanation probably lies in the use of gas as an illuminant. Begonias were always very sensitive to the fumes from coal gas and tended to drop their leaves if exposed to such fumes for long. The fumes from North Sea gas seem less lethal to begonias, although they still do not really like them. One would have thought that the Victorians could have grown them in their closed cases, and maybe they did, but failed to mention the fact.

Nowadays central heating may keep houses as warm in winter as the warmest greenhouse, with the result that it is possible to grow in our houses plants formerly only grown in the warmest greenhouses that were known as stoves, and it is with these warmth-loving subjects that our century can show a larger number of plants than would have been possible in the 1870s.

Mind you, most of the modern house plants were being grown in Victorian greenhouses. John Gould Veitch had brought back a large selection of crotons from his voyage in Polynesia in 1863, and also many choice sorts of *Cordyline terminalis*. The Belgian Linden, who had himself collected plants when in South America, sent out collectors to that continent and it is to them that we owe many of the philodendrons that were so popular until quite recently and which are not neglected even now. Most of these were introduced to cultivation in the 1880s, although some had been around longer. Peperomias were better known. The popular Rugby football plant, *P. argyreia*, arrived in 1866, while *P. obtusifolia* had been in cultivation since 1817. *Aphelandra squarrosa* seems to have been known since the end of the 1860s, while 1874 saw the introduction of *A. fascinator*, which looks to be the most desirable of the genus, but which awaits reintroduction. Dieffenbachias arrived mainly in the 1870s. At this time there was a noted hybridist called Bausé, for whose services different British nurseries used to vie, and it would seem that it is to him that we owe many of our modern sorts of *Cordyline terminalis* and some of the more brilliant forms of *Dieffenbachia picta*. There still survives a dieffenbachia known as 'Bausei'. One would dearly like to know more about this master apart from a few scattered references in gardening journals of the 1870s and 1880s.

Mother-in-law's tongue, *Sansevieria*, has been grown since the eighteenth century, although it must have been comparatively recently that the variegated 'Laurentii' arose. One of the first Australian plants to get into cultivation was *Cissus antarctica*, the kangaroo vine, although it does not seem to have been very highly thought of until recently. Still, you could have grown it at the end of the eighteenth century. Oddly enough the first *Cordyline terminalis* arrived in Europe as long ago as 1771, when it was brought from China, of all unlikely places. If the Chinese were growing it so long ago it must already have been considerably developed. It was originally called *Dracaena ferrea*. Most of the calatheas came into cultivation between 1850 and 1880, but *C. zebrina* was as early as 1817 and the popular and variable *C. ornata* arrived in 1849.

Possibly as a reaction against an excess of brilliant bedding, the later Victorians developed a great love for attractive foliage and several volumes with names like *Beautiful-leaved Plants* were published. They also liked very large leaves. There was a reaction against flower bedding in the sub-tropical garden, which was created in Paris in the 1850s and which was increasingly popular as the century advanced. In this not only coloured leaves were appreciated – it was the heyday of plants such as caladiums and Rex begonias -- but also plants with very large leaves were in demand. Most of these plants are no longer to be seen. *Wigandia caracasana* and *Montanoa bipinnatifida* could once have been purchased from any good nursery, but there can be few nowadays who have ever seen them. There used to be a selection of large-leaved solanums, their leaves often decorated with yellow spines, and they too have vanished as house plants. Another genus which the liking for large leaves brought into cultivation was *Schefflera*. I doubt whether it included the *S. actinophylla* we grow as a house plant nowadays, but it is not impossible.

On parts of the continent *Chlorophytum comosum* is known as the Goethe plant, as its viviparous nature so fascinated Goethe (who fancied himself as a botanist, though with little justification) that he distributed plants to all his friends. Of the other most popular and easiest of house plants we seem to

Sansevieria trifasciata laurentii

Ficus elastica

Saintpaulia

Tradescantia fluminensis

know little as to when they came into cultivation. *Zebrina pendula* was certainly around in 1850, but I think the variegated tradescantias must be comparatively recent. One is mentioned in a book of 1885, with no suggestion that it was particularly new, but most writers I know seem reluctant to mention them at all. An enormous number of unvariegated tradescantias were in cultivation by 1830, although it is by no means certain if they included *T. albiflora* and *T. fluminensis*, but until variegated forms had developed one would not have expected them to attract any interest.

Although the bulk of our house plants have been in cultivation for a century, there are some which have only been introduced quite recently. The shrimp plant, *Beloperone*, was only brought from Mexico in 1936, while the aluminium plant, *Pilea cadieri*, was introduced in 1938 and it is thought that the millions of plants now growing all derive vegetatively from this introduction. Since the plant came from Vietnam, which is not a region that has been conducive to botanical exploration since 1938, there seems nothing unlikely in the story. Some mutations do seem to have arisen however, as one or two cultivars are now available.

If this article has a moral it is that very little in gardening is as modern as we might think. Most of us have always thought that the popularity of house plants was a post-war fashion and one that depended a great deal on the availability of central heating. This certainly should be true, but unfortunately neither humans nor plants will always behave logically. Probably research would find an eighteenth-century cult of house plants. I hope someone does, but I am afraid it will not be me.

Gardening
in Retirement

Ralph E. Thoday, V.M.H.

Vinca minor   *Pachysandra terminalis*

S OME YEARS ago I spoke to a garden student meeting on 'Planning for Retirement' but I fear it was not much appreciated. Now, with personal experience behind me, I realize even more that this subject must be considered seriously well before one has reached the half-century mark.

When one reaches the age of retirement there is often a resurgence of energy from the excitement that now there is ample time to do everything. Not infrequently however, within perhaps six months, the reason for a fixed retirement age dawns upon us, assisted by ills and wear of the human body. So I would say prepare as early as possible for an enjoyable retirement into a garden of one's own design, with dreamed-of flowering plants, vegetables and fruits.

Before retirement some of us may be fortunate enough to find a house and garden satisfactory to our tastes and wishes, one that is beyond the imaginative description of house agents. I would suggest, however, that alterations are nearly always necessary for pensioners. Not infrequently a drastic reduction of trees and shrubs, especially tall apple trees, pears or plums, will be necessary. These respond to shortening by sending out new lower growth, which again should be reduced after a year or two to the number and size required; in the case of the leader to replace the removed bough, this should be cut by half the current year's growth. This operation should be repeated annually until the tree has reached the desired size. By the way, if any large boughs are removed by sawing, always smooth the rough surface and paint over with Arbrex or a similar wound preparation to reduce the risk of spores of silverleaf and other diseases entering the wound. In this way we can have fruit trees of reasonable size and height, easy for gathering the fruits in due season. Flowering shrubs can also be curtailed, but one seldom finds this is necessary.

Not only trees need keeping within manageable size; indeed, hedges usually provide the major chore. If a new hedge is to be planted, try the field maple (*Acer campestre*); it has a pleasing colour, needs minimum trimming and has the advantage of being deep-rooted and so not robbing nearby plants of food and water, unlike the popular privet. Conifers are popular nowadays, rapidly providing all the essential privacy where houses are close together or overlook each other. Two of the best are Leyland cypress (× *Cupressocyparis leylandii*) and Western red cedar (*Thuya plicata*). Never cramp them in the mistaken idea that they will form a closer hedge; 4 ft between the plants is enough. *Berberis* × *stenophylla* makes a useful barrier hedge, is quick-growing, flowers attractively and needs only light pruning after the blossoming period in mid-June. Hedges to divide one section of the garden from another can be composed of cordon trees such as apple, pear and plum.

Attention must be given to the lawn, perhaps to clear out weeds and moss. My advice is to wait until the grass starts to grow in March. Raking moss with a wire rake is the usual advice, but this is very tiring work and much research work has been done on chemicals which can be obtained from garden centres and sundriesmen. Weed killers also now come in bottles and are very effective, but must be applied according to makers' instructions. Before sowing a new lawn there is much to be said for preparing the site with well-rotted manure or compost and then to grow a crop of early potatoes which can be lifted and cleared before August or September. This will clear the soil of any remaining weeds at just the right time to sow the seed. Make a good job of the levelling and firming and select a good seed strain from a reliable seedsman. Seed can be sown at the rate of 1-1½ oz to the sq. yd and should be weighed out correctly. Seed can be treated with a bird repellent and again used according to makers' instructions. The surface can then be scratched with an iron rake in two directions to make sure the seed is covered. The next operation is to roll the surface with a light roller; if lucky with showers, germination will be prompt. Before any early winter frosts are expected the grass should be ready for a trim with a well-adjusted and sharp mower. Of course if it can be afforded by a pensioner in these expensive days, laying a good turf is ideal and quick.

Older folk seem to me to get particular satisfaction from a good kitchen garden. It is very nice indeed to enjoy one's own vegetables and salads. Work is made easier by dividing the vegetable plot into three parts. Section one should be nearest the dwelling house and contain ideally but not essentially a greenhouse, a shed, frames and/or cloches and a compost heap. Section two should grow brassicas (greens of all kinds), section three for potatoes and the perennial vegetables such as the three types of artichokes, seakale, rhubarb and horseradish. Space also for a row of spinach and runner beans must be reserved. If the crops are rotated, diseases are kept at a minimum and the best use is made of the available soil minerals.

I must stress the great importance of the compost heap. Any living vegetable material should be decomposed within the heap. All green plants such as nettles, grass and weeds will do this, especially if it is possible to add small quantities of such animal droppings as from poultry. A small amount of water added over each layer of material will, when covered with 2 in. of garden soil, start rapid bacterial action. If made properly the heap will heat up sufficiently to kill pests and weed seeds.

If a front garden needs to be cultivated, then this can be planted with roses of personal choice. I am perhaps old-fashioned in thinking that violas are the perfect border edge here, and my memories go back to a lovely variety called 'Maggie Mott' and a multi-coloured smaller-flowered strain called 'Jackanapes'. Seeds can still be bought of the latter but the named cultivars are not so easy to come by. Until 1975 violas were a great feature at North Country shows and displayed in special glass stands. The competition was very strong and the judges severe in their treatment of this particular section. There are other fine plants of course that will show off a front garden; geraniums and fuchsias are very popular . . . but there, this is your choice. I do know of a remarkably successful front garden where Dad has top-quality tuberous

Narcissus pseudonarcissus

Berberis x stenophylla

begonias from home-grown seed, and Mum has her half of mixed flowers. The display of the two halves harmonizes to the pleasure of the family and pleases passers-by.

The herbaceous border is a subject in itself but is not beyond the powers of the pensioner if those more sturdy plants that need no staking are used and when the spaces (if any) are filled with hardy or half-hardy annuals. A beautiful coloured border is a delight and personally I never worry about the possibility of colours clashing. Early April is usually a good time to plant when, as with most hardy plants, the roots are active. To transplant when the plant is dormant or when the soil is very cold is to court disaster. For all beds and borders, a good annual mulching of well-decayed horse or farmyard manure is a tremendous spur to growth. Some public gardeners I know dig up and divide their herbaceous borders each year, others thin by planting every third year. During this operation the young outer portions of the plants are replaced into soil enriched with well-decayed farmyard manure, preferably cow for sandy soil and horse for the more retentive clay type. The choicest specimens in the border such as delphiniums, phlox and poppies should not be split up but replaced by young plants from cuttings when the clumps become less vigorous. If the chore of digging and re-planting is not appreciated, then either choose perennials which seldom need dividing or replacing, e.g. *Astilbe, Cimicifuga, Dictamnus albus, Campanula lactiflora*, perennial sorts of *Eryngium* and all peonies, or use shrubs instead. A good idea is to plant the smaller, more compact shrubs rather closer together than the reference books recommend. In a few years they will touch and form a pleasing weed-smothering mosaic. If there is enough room for the taller shrubs these can be used in the same way. Alternatively each shrub can be given plenty of space to develop as a specimen, the space between filled with good evergreen ground-cover such as *Vinca minor* or *Pachysandra terminalis*. It is important that enough ground-cover plants to fill the chosen area should be set out at one go. Doing the job piecemeal over an extended period is never satisfactory, allowing weeds to spring up in the bare areas.

To avoid the common mistake of using plants unsuitable for the area, shrubs can be selected after a close inspection of those growing well in the district and therefore suitable for your soil. This I find is just what some of the commercial landscapers do. Do remember that such admirable plants as rhododendrons and other acid-lovers will not tolerate chalk.

If one's garden is a large one there may be room to have a real natural garden, with very reasonable upkeep. Here trees are planted thinly to allow light to penetrate to the massed bulbs and small plants below. A wonderful example of what I mean is the Wilderness Garden at St John's College, Cambridge, the design of which is attributed to 'Capability' Brown and which can be viewed from Queens Road. Here, masses of aconites, crocus, especially of course the Cambridge blue *C. tomasinianus*, snowdrops and snowflakes together with other bulbs flower from February to July. The naturalized

Narcissus pseudonarcissus is followed in June by masses of *Lilium martagon*. The secret of this quiet sanctuary is that all the plants are allowed to set and ripen their seeds and not until August to the end of October are they subjected to just one big cut-over by scythe or mower set high.

For those who start a garden from scratch after retirement, there are many ideas and tools which lighten the initial work and make maintenance easier. Among tools a spring-loaded spade makes for easier digging and there are several lightweight hoes and hand cultivators. As the back gets less supple and the gardener uses his knees to get down to ground level, a good pair of knee-pads is a must. By organizing the garden properly some of the tedious and/or back-breaking chores can be reduced or eliminated. If the garden is on a slope, make sure there are no steps to stumble on. Contour the paths gently and if stone is used make sure it is not slippery in wet weather.

For the unfortunate few who find themselves confined to a wheelchair, this need not be the end of gardening. Restricting one's interest to greenhouse plants on benches at the right height is an obvious idea. In the open garden, raised beds are the solution. These can have walls of brick, artificial or natural stone or old railway sleepers built to the desired height. Make sure that each bed is of a width that can be easily weeded or cultivated to the centre from either side. Such beds are ideal for rock and alpine plants, but all plants that need well-drained soil will thrive, not least the vegetables.

Visiting Gardens

John G. Scott Marshall, N.D.H. (Hons.)

Stourhead

NAPOLEON is said to have described the English as a nation of shopkeepers; he would probably have been nearer the mark if he had said gardeners. Just why the English should have such a passion for gardening is hard to decide. It probably relates to the fact that for generations our ancestors tilled the soil and so, intangibly, inculcated a love of the open air, of nature and of gardens which persists to this day. Yet another intangible aspect of the English is their ability to produce gifted amateurs; few arts or crafts have benefited more from the activities of such people than gardening.

Gardens cannot be considered in isolation but only in relation to the people who made them, and one of the fascinations of visiting gardens is to meet their owners. Alas, once the owner has gone, only too quickly the garden follows suit. Gardens are ephemeral and how sad it is to see a neglected garden that once was loved and tended. Fortunately there are organizations, like the National Trust and the Garden History Society, which can be relied upon to come to the rescue by either looking after gardens of special merit, or serving as a pressure group for their preservation and maintenance. Such organizations deserve our whole-hearted support, especially in times of roaring inflation. A growing awareness of this problem for the future of English gardens is shown by the following extract entitled 'Danger – Taxes at Work' taken from the booklet *Gardens of England and Wales Open to the Public – 1979*, published by the National Gardens Scheme: 'Inflation has not only raised the cost of maintaining a garden several times, it has also reduced the value of whatever capital may still be available to support the larger gardens. Indeed, the weight and inescapability of capital taxation now makes it almost impossible for a succeeding generation to keep up the standards of the past. The alternative of transfer to the National Trust is only available in a very few cases, since the capital endowment needed in any inflationary age is beyond the means of most owners.

'Our greatest gardens cannot survive for long under present-day taxation without relief. If you care about conservation, support the national amenity societies in their efforts to obtain reliefs and grants to hold our great heritage of gardens intact.'

With over 1,500 gardens open in 1979 in England and Wales, and 232 in Scotland plus those in Ireland, there are obviously more people than ever before enjoying the hobby of garden visiting. Why there should be this growing interest must surely relate to the infinite variety the subject offers. For some it will be the escape from the claustrophobic atmosphere of the office, town or city; the fresh air and sweet smells of growing plants, of bird song, wind in the trees, the play of light and shade on smooth grass and perhaps the sound of running water; for others, the inexhaustible study of plant life in all its infinite variety from trees to alpines. For the lucky ones it is an amalgam of all these things plus an appreciation of social history which over the centuries has fashioned our gardens into what they are today, often a conglomeration of two or even three styles.

The history of gardening need not be a boring methodical record of past events, but rather a fascinating study of how a garden has changed and developed over the years, and of the people who brought those changes about. We know that the English only really started to make gardens in the seventeenth century and then to emulate the French and Italians with very formal designs. At Oxburgh Hall near King's Lynn, Norfolk there is a French parterre garden to the east of the red brick mansion, while in Scotland at Drummond Castle, Crieff, Perthshire, there is an Italian formal garden. At Hardwick Hall, Doe Lea, Chesterfield, Derbyshire – built for the much-married Bess of Hardwick (Dowager Countess of Shrewsbury) in 1597 – there are formal and walled courtyard gardens. Packwood House, Lapworth, Solihull, Warwickshire – a timber-framed Tudor house with mid-seventeenth-century additions – has a Caroline formal garden and a mid-seventeenth-century yew garden representing the Sermon on the Mount. The knot garden at Little Moreton Hall, Congleton, Cheshire – a fifteenth-century 'black-and-white' moated house – is typical of the period, as is the box knot garden with plants of the period at Moseley Old Hall, Fordhouses, Wolverhampton. In the south at Lytes Cary, Somerton, Somerset – once the home of Henry Lyte, the author of *Niewe Herball* (1578) – there are very old formal hedges. The National Trust has recently restored the seventeenth-century garden at Ham House, Richmond, Surrey to a plan dated 1670, and formal gardens are also to be seen at Gunby Hall, Gunby, near Spilsby, Lincolnshire; Ickworth, Bury St Edmunds, Suffolk; and at Montacute House, near Yeovil, Somerset.

In Scotland at the now ruined castle of Edzell, Tayside, Angus – once associated with the ill-fated Mary, Queen of Scots – the well-preserved walled garden dates from 1604. The garden at Pitmedden, near Udny, Grampian – founded in 1675 – has been restored using the elaborate floral designs of the period. The yew hedges at Crathes Castle, Grampian, Kincardineshire, are said to date from 1702; the formal garden at Brodick Castle, Isle of Arran, Strathclyde, from 1710; and the walled garden at the Culzean Country Park, Strathclyde, from 1783.

Such early enclosed gardens often had a mound from which the occupants of the establishment could look down on the geometrical designs of the garden, but perhaps more importantly look out beyond the protective walls to a time of greater freedom. When at last peace and prosperity came, the castle gradually became a villa, and the garden escaped confinement and spread out into the surrounding country. Although defence considerations were by then no longer paramount, barren sites were selected for building because of the scope they gave for vast formal plantations. Long alleys, made with yew, beech or lime, carried the eye to infinity. Even water was made to conform to this pattern by the construction of canal-like pools. The earliest garden of this kind remaining in England is Westbury Court, Westbury-on-Severn, Gloucestershire, originally laid out between 1696 and 1705, and restored by the National Trust in 1971. Other gardens of this period are at Hampton Court

Chatsworth

Palace, Chertsey, Surrey – which also has a Tudor knot garden; Chatsworth, Derbyshire; and Wrest Park, Silsoe, near Bedford, where the long water forms an axis and a pavilion its most prominent feature. The pavilion is one of the best examples of garden architecture in the country, designed by Thomas Archer in 1709-11, and decorated by Nicholas Hauduroy, an artist from the Low Countries. It is, like the whole garden and the other buildings it contains, in a good state of repair. A column in the woods, which have many vistas and rides, records that 'These gardens were begun in the year 1706 by the Duke of Kent who continued to beautify them until the year 1740: Philip, Earl of Hardwick and Jemima, Marchioness de Grey, with the professional assistance of Lancelot Brown Esq 1758-1760'.

If you take an interest in garden history it is not long before you encounter Lancelot 'Capability' Brown (1716-83). He is often criticized (as recently as in the exhibition '1,000 Years of Gardening' at the Victoria and Albert Museum) for the part he played in the eighteenth-century destruction of gardens when parks were literally brought right up to the walls of great houses; a possibility facilitated by Charles Bridgeman's use of the haha, an adaption of the military revetment, to exclude cattle from the precincts of the house.

This remarkable revolution in English garden design took place as a result of boredom or perhaps disenchantment with the restrictions of the formal garden. Attention was focused on Nature as idealized by painters, poets and writers; gardens were created to inspire a sense of awe and to exploit the genius of the place. Sites of varying levels, previously eschewed, were selected, and natural beauty enhanced by the construction of carefully sited garden buildings, at first classical and romantic in design but later more fanciful and even curious.

The earliest surviving English landscape garden – Claremont, Esher, Surrey – begun by Vanbrugh and Bridgeman before 1720, and later extended and naturalized by Kent, has recently been restored by the National Trust. The present house, designed in 1772 for Clive of India by Henry Holland and Lancelot Brown (wearing his architect's hat), replaced a house built by Vanbrugh for his own occupation. Clive of India is also associated with Powis Castle, Welshpool, famous for its mediaeval castle and its early eighteenth-century terraced garden. Sheffield Park, Uckfield, East Sussex – a garden of five lakes laid out in the eighteenth century – is worth visiting in spring for the rhododendron blossom, and in autumn for the leaf colour of the deciduous trees. Stourhead, Stourton, Warminster, Wiltshire – laid out by Sir Henry Hoare between 1741 and 1750 – is one of our finest landscaped gardens. Scotney Castle, Lamberhurst, Kent, with a garden made round the ruins of a fourteenth-century moated castle, is one of the most picturesque and romantic, while Alton Towers in Staffordshire – home of the Earls of Shrewsbury – exemplifies the excesses of the later period.

At Blenheim Palace, Woodstock, Oxfordshire; Bowood, Calne, Wiltshire; and Petworth House, Petworth, West Sussex, the planting strove to marry the garden into the landscape so successfully that it is difficult now for us to see where the work of the garden-maker ends and nature takes over. Lancelot Brown worked at Blenheim Palace in the 1760s, and it is regarded as his grandest, if not his finest work. He was employed at Petworth and at Bowood, where he was succeeded by Humphrey Repton (1752-1818), but the parkland there today remains much as Brown left it. Wimpole Hall, near New Wimpole, Cambridgeshire – a property not long in the hands of the National Trust – has a park landscaped by Bridgeman, Brown and Repton.

The nineteenth century saw plant-collecting from all parts of the world, and it says much for the temperate English climate that so many took root and flourished. For plants that would tolerate the winter, herbaceous borders were established, such as those at Arley Hall, Cheshire; Pusey House near Oxford; and in Scotland at Falkland Palace, Fife, and Leith Hall, Kennethmont, Grampian. For woody plants shrubberies, arboretums and pinetums were planted, and the overall effect on garden design was dramatic. The Westonbirt Arboretum, Tetbury, Gloucestershire was founded by Robert Stayner Halford in 1829; it is now part of a 600-acre Forestry Commission estate. At the historic Scottish palace of Scone, Tayside, Perthshire, and at the Bedgebury National Pinetum, Flimwell, Kent (established by the Forestry Commission in 1925) the most comprehensive collections of conifers in Europe can be seen. The pinetum at Scone was started in 1848 and has in its collection a Douglas fir raised from the original seed sent from America in 1834 by David Douglas, at one time a worker on the estate.

The botanic gardens have always been actively involved in plant distribution, and established collections of plants, trees and shrubs (with labels!) are to be seen throughout the year in delightful surroundings at the Royal Botanic Gardens, Kew, Richmond, Surrey – within twenty miles of the centre of London. The Oxford University Botanic Garden, High Street (by Magdalen Bridge), established in 1621, was the first botanic garden to be started in England. The university arboretum is at Nuneham Courteney. The Cambridge University Botanic Garden was founded in 1762, though not at its present site on the Trumpington Road. The Bristol University Botanic Garden, Bracken Hill, and the University of Liverpool Botanic Garden, Ness, Wirral, started as the gardens of a keen amateur gardener, Arthur Kilpin Bulley. He gave financial support to, among others the famous collectors of Himalayan plants, George Forrest and Frank Kingdon-Ward. It was in the catalogues of the firm Bees Ltd – started by Bulley – that the public were offered for the first time in 1909-13 seeds of many of the new plants found by his collectors. Cities that support botanic gardens include Bath, Birmingham, Liverpool and Sheffield.

In Scotland the Royal Botanic Garden, Inverleith Row, Edinburgh is renowed for its rock garden, rhododendrons and modern approach to glasshouse design. Others are the Younger Botanic Garden, Benmore, Strathclyde, Argyll, a woodland garden on a grand scale; the Dawyck

Arboretum, Peeblesshire, an out-station of the Royal Botanic Garden; the Logan Botanic Garden, near Ardwell, Stranraer, the home of cabbage palms and Australian gums; and the Glasgow Botanic Garden on the Great Western Road, whose collections include one of tree ferns housed in the Kibble Palace.

In the Victorian era the practice of 'bedding out' reached a pinnacle of perfection. Winter-sensitive plants were taken under glass and hot-water heating systems used to keep out the cold and to enable the vast numbers of half-hardy plants to be propagated as the elaborate bedding schemes demanded. Bedding out is still popular in seaside resorts and at such spa towns as Bath, Leamington and Harrogate, though the rising cost of fuel must throw some doubt on the future.

Climate and soil combined in Cornwall and the west of Scotland to make possible the woodland garden, which in the first instance grew rhododendrons and azaleas, but soon included the wide variety of plants that thrive in thin woodland and on acid soil. Today many regard the woodland garden as peculiarly English, an attitude no doubt fostered by the replicas of the Royal Horticultural Society's garden at Wisley, Surrey staged at Chelsea Flower Show and at similar exhibitions in Europe with remarkable success. The hall-mark of these gardens is the quality and variety of planting, and the fact that grown naturally and in a conducive environment, plants will often establish and regenerate themselves so well as to require the minimum of attention with regard to maintenance.

Outstanding gardens of this kind are to be seen in the Sussex Weald, namely Nymans, Handcross, Haywards Heath; Leonardslee, Lower Beeding; Wakehurst Palace, Ardingly; and Sheffield Park, midway between East Grinstead and Lewes, East Sussex. There are also the Savill Garden (Windsor Great Park) reached via Wick Lane, Englefield Green, near Egham, Berkshire; Hever Castle, Hever, Kent; Killerton, Devon; Knightshayes, Tiverton, Devon; Dartington Hall, Devon; Lanhydrock, Bodmin, Cornwall; Trengwainton, Heamor, near Penzance, Cornwall; Bodnant near Llandudno, north Wales; Harlow Car, Crag Lane, Otley Road, Harrogate, North Yorkshire; Cragside, Rothbury, Northumberland; and in Scotland two gardens not previously mentioned, Achamore, Isle of Gigha, Argyll, and Inverewe, Poolewe, Highland (Ross and Cromarty).

Many gardens of the present century reflect the ideas first expounded by William Robinson and Gertrude Jekyll, often working in association with the architect Sir Edwin Lutyens. Their planting schemes emphasized the colour and form, not only of the flowers but of the leaves. The essential element of surprise in garden design returned, and large gardens were made that consisted of several smaller ones each complete in itself. Examples include Hidcote Manor, Mickleton, Gloucestershire, created by Major Lawrence Johnston, and Sissinghurst Castle near Cranbrook, Kent, designed by Sir Harold Nicolson and his wife Victoria Sackville-West.

One of the fascinations of British gardens is their extraordinary variety, but as tastes in gardening are as varied as in everything else, prospective visitors would be well advised to avoid disappointment by selecting the gardens they think that they will like, before setting out, using the many books or descriptive lists available. The following titles should be in every garden visitor's library, but remember to check the details of opening with a reliable authority, such as the local National Tourist Information Centre, *before* setting off.

Gardens of the National Trust by Graham Stuart Thomas, published by Weidenfeld and Nicolson, £9.95.

The Gardens of Britain (Vols 1-6), published by Batsford at £6.50 each volume.

The Shell Guide to Gardens, published by William Heinemann Ltd, £2.95.

Historic Houses, Castles and Gardens in Great Britain and Ireland, published annually in January by ABC Historic Publications, 60p, available from booksellers or from the publishers at Oldhill, London Road, Dunstable, Beds, 96p including packing and postage.

Castles and Historic Houses, Gardens and Places of Interest Open to the Public, published by the Royal Automobile Club and available from booksellers, £2.25, or the RAC plus 25p for packing and postage.

Stately Homes, Museums, Castles and Gardens in Britain, published by the Automobile Association, £1.95 to non-members, and available from AA bookshops or direct from Fanum House, Basingstoke, Hants RG21 2EA.

Gardens Open to the Public in England and Wales, published annually by the National Gardens Scheme, and available direct from 57 Lower Belgrave Street, London SW1W 0LR, 75p including packing and postage, or 50p from booksellers.

Gardens to Visit, published annually by the Gardeners' Sunday Organization and obtainable direct from White Witches, Claygate Road, Dorking, Surrey, 35p including packing and postage, or 25p from booksellers.

The National Trust — Gardens Open In England, Wales and Northern Ireland, available from 42 Queen Anne's Gate, London SW1H 9AS, 30p, or from booksellers 20p.

The National Trust for Scotland — Gardens to Visit, available from 5 Charlotte Square, Edinburgh EH2 4DK, 55p including packing and postage.

Scotland's Gardens, published annually by Scotland's Gardens Scheme, 26 Castle Terrace, Edinburgh EH1 2EL, 55p including packing and postage, or 40p from booksellers.

The Historic Irish Tourist Houses and Gardens Association makes available a descriptive list of about 40 gardens that is available from Fred's Travel Bureau, 3a Castle Street, Dalkey, Co. Dublin.

Castles and Historic Places in Wales, available from the Wales Tourist Board, PO Box 151, WDO, Cardiff CF5 1XS, 80p plus 20p packing and postage.

Garden Britain Observer Map, £1.25, published by Map Productions Ltd, 27a Floral Street, London WC2E 9LP.

No discussion about gardens would be complete without an

acknowledgement of the debt owed to gardeners, without whom none of the works of art we savour today would have been possible. Many a garden owed its very existence to the devoted care, especially in times of national crisis, of those whose names are nowhere recorded. Unfortunately in making this acknowledgement it has to be admitted that gardening has always been a low-paid profession, and that too often appalling hardship has been suffered by those – gardeners all their lives – who when they became too old to work were often faced with extreme deprivation or the workhouse.

Late in 1838 a group of growers met in London to discuss this problem under the chairmanship of one George Glenny, and the result was the establishment of the Gardeners' Benevolent Institution. An appeal for funds was launched to nurserymen, seedsmen and to the gardeners of noblemen and gentlemen, happily with an encouraging response, though it was two years before enough money had been collected to make possible the payment of the first pension. Matters improved when Queen Victoria became patron, a tradition that persists to this day when Queen Elizabeth the Queen Mother is patron, and Princess Alice, Duchess of Gloucester, the current president. In 1852 the Institution gave a festival dinner presided over by Charles Dickens, and characteristically he is recorded as saying when speaking of the needs of gardeners: 'His gains are not great and he knows gold and silver more as being the colours of fruit and flowers than by their presence in his pockets. He is subjected to that kind of labour which renders him peculiarly liable to infirmity, and when old age comes upon him the gardener is, of all men perhaps, best able to appreciate the benefits of the Institution.' The passage of time has done little to change the validity of these words, even though we may now live in a welfare state. Today there are 360 pensioners and about 60 old people being cared for in the home at Henfield, Sussex, or in bungalows run by the society. Now in its 140th year, the society is located at Palace Gate, Hampton Court, East Molesey, Surrey KT8 9BN, and still depends on voluntary contributions to be able to continue its work.

The Gardeners' Sunday Organization, the charity that since 1956 has done so much to encourage garden visits, supports both the Gardeners' Royal Benevolent Society and the Royal Gardeners' Orphan Fund – so far to the tune of £186,522. The latter was established in 1887 to commemorate the Golden Jubilee of Queen Victoria and makes regular allowances or special grants to the orphans of gardeners. Although the demand for such help was greatest when there were many gardeners in private service, and especially when a family which lived in a tied cottage lost the breadwinner, help is still needed today by gardeners in the public sector even though the widow and family may be found a council house.

The Constance Spry Fund, set up in 1960 to commemorate her work and inspiration, also exists to help the orphans of gardeners, especially those who have the chance of further education but cannot afford to take it. The fund operates from the same address as the Royal Gardeners' Orphan Fund, at 46

St Albans Road, Codicote, Hitchin, Herts SG4 8UT, and both charities welcome subscriptions or donations to further their work.

As we look to the future the continued popularity of visiting gardens would seem to be assured; only the energy crisis and the possibility of petrol rationing cast an ominous shadow. With more than 1,450 gardens open in England and Wales, of which 1,250 are private and not usually open to the public, the National Gardens Scheme, operating from 57 Lower Belgrave Street, London SW1W 0LR, is obviously tapping enormous good-will among gardeners and coping magnificently with the demand which has grown steadily since 1927, when the scheme started in the memory of Queen Alexandra to continue the development of the district nursing service and care for nurses in retirement. Miss Elsie Wagg, a member of council of the Queen's Institute, pointed out that this country was renowned for its gardens but that few people ever had the opportunity to see them; she suggested that the owners might be persuaded to arrange an open day on behalf of the Queen's Institute. In that first spring and summer of 1927 over 600 gardens were opened, with large numbers of people enjoying what was then a unique opportunity of seeing what was on the other side of the wall.

Today opening has become an accepted routine for gardens big and small; it is even helping to keep some very famous gardens in existence. Among the charities that benefit from garden openings are the British Red Cross Society, St John Ambulance, and the Soldiers', Sailors' and Airmen's Families Association. The garden-visiting public and the charity organizations are greatly indebted to those who willingly shoulder the burden of opening their gardens year after year, and to those who give of their time to help on the day. Economically, politically and socially Britain has changed beyond recognition since Charles Dickens deplored the fate of gardeners in old age, or Miss Elsie Wagg launched the National Gardens Scheme, but through all these changes the love of nature, gardens and plants has survived; long may it continue to do so for the benefit of all concerned.